Anomalous:
The Adventures of Sherlock Holmes featuring Jack Johnson and Alphonse Capone

Samuel Williams, Jr.

First edition published in 2012

© Copyright 2012
Samuel Williams, Jr.

The right of Samuel Williams, Jr. to be identified as the author of this work has been asserted by him in accordance with the Copyright, Designs and Patents Act 1998.

All rights reserved. No reproduction, copy or transmission of this publication may be made without express prior written permission. No paragraph of this publication may be reproduced, copied or transmitted except with express prior written permission or in accordance with the provisions of the Copyright Act 1956 (as amended). Any person who commits any unauthorised act in relation to this publication may be liable to criminal prosecution and civil claims for damage.

All characters appearing in this work are fictitious. Any resemblance to real persons, living or dead, is purely coincidental. The opinions expressed herein are those of the author and not of MX Publishing.

Paperback ISBN 978-1-78092-259-1
ePub ISBN 978-1-78092-260-7
PDF ISBN 978-1-78092-261-4

Published in the UK by MX Publishing
335 Princess Park Manor, Royal Drive,
London, N11 3GX
www.mxpublishing.com

Cover design by www.staunch.com

Dedicated to Roberta Taliaferro, Raymond and Clarisse Burrell.

Acknowledgments

I thank my Lord and Saviour, Jesus Christ, who blessed me with the opportunity to publish this book. I serve an awesome God!

I extend a huge salute to MX Publishing based in London, England who had the incredible faith in me to publish *Anomalous*. I extend a huge thanks to my wife, Valerie, who when all others doubted me, remained steadfast with faith in me. And a heartfelt thanks my editor Barbara McLay and Chico Norwood my proof reader and researcher.

Thanks to my mother, Letitia Williams, who never allowed me to doubt what I could achieve. Thanks to Louis Randall and Christchurch School, the tiny private, Episcopalian boarding school located on the banks of the Rappahannock River in Middlesex, County (Virginia) for an awesome education. Virtus, Veritas and Fortitudo!

Thanks to Linda Soucek, my former elementary school teacher, and God bless you with a speedy recovery.

Thanks Samuel Williams, Sr., Renee Selden, Jess Hinson, Betty Coleman, Rev. George Morris, Dr. Debbie Stroman, Patricia Selden, Sheila Jackson and Tina Sims for your encouragement.

Thanks for the spiritual support from my church family at Dunamis Power Christian Fellowship in San Bernardino, California.

I hope this book will inspire my granddaughters; Jada Williams, London and Morgan Ashford as well as my godsons; Julian, Timothy and Jackson Jamerson, to love Jesus Christ and fall in love with the craft of writing. I also thank my two sons; JaVon Samuel Williams and Ryan Christopher Williams for being inspirations. Lastly, I thank Gregory Selden, who will help market the book in North America.

A final note: Any mistakes in this book are mine, and mine alone.

Contents

Prologue	1
Chapter 1	3
Chapter 2	16
Chapter 3	38
Chapter 4	49
Chapter 5	61
Chapter 6	76
Chapter 7	82
Chapter 8	98
Chapter 9	107
Chapter 10	117
Chapter 11	131
Chapter 12	144
Chapter 13	158
Chapter 14	171
Epilogue	185

Prologue

As the five men entered the street adjoining the alley, the scene was pandemonium. Three men had three ropes around Johnson's upper torso trapping his arms.

"You gents weren't lying," Kessler said as he watched the hapless Jack Johnson being led to a sturdy lamppost. Altamont, in yet another disguise, stood on a stepladder next to the lamppost with a rope skilfully knotted with a noose dangling at the end.

Yale whispered to Capone. "This is way too real," Yale said. Unknowing to Johnson, Yale, and perhaps even Capone, they had grown attached to the colored man they were sent to protect. The fear in Johnson's eyes was real. Real in the since that the threesome, who had Johnson attached to their ropes, were not privy to the elaborate scheme that had been devised to set up this scenario. Their racist demeanour and rants were from the heart. Yale wanted to pull his snub-nosed revolver and save Johnson, but he trusted Altamont, so he stayed true to script.

"Okay, you two stay in the shadows," Yale said as he handed Kessler his revolver. "I'll stay with you until they hang him and The Weasel, returns with the keys."

Kessler and Wilson nodded and stayed in the shadows with Yale. Capone and The Weasel went to join the crowd. As they neared the scene, the stench of men seeking death was thick, convincing. Capone, made his way to the noose and beckoned for the three men holding Johnson captive to come to him. Capone fitted the noose around Johnson's neck, exactly as Altamont had instructed. Altamont tied the other end of the rope to a hansom and instructed the driver to pull forward.

Johnson's huge body was lifted to the very top of the lamppost, and per Altamont's instructions, Johnson kicked his legs violently and then went still. It was easy to do for Johnson, since he had witnessed a hanging as a child in Texas. He kept his eyes closed and didn't move. Because he was so high, and because of the darkness and distance to the alley shadow in which Kessler and Wilson were hidden, as best they could tell Johnson was dead.

The men in the lynching party laid hold to Johnson's possessions, and Capone stood in front of them. "I'm selling this dead man's possessions," Capone said loudly. "I'll start with his keys. Any buyers?"

"Fifty American dollars for the dead man's keys," The Weasel said, true to script.

"They're yours, my friend," Capone said. He went to The Weasel and collected the cash.

"I get my money back, right?" The Weasel whispered.

"In your dreams," Capone whispered back. The Weasel, cursed Capone under his breath, as he ran to the three figures in the alley. He handed the keys to Wilson.

"We're gone," Wilson exclaimed with glee, as he handed Yale his revolver, and made haste, behind Kessler, to the waiting hansom. Yale followed them to make sure they left. He returned to the street.

"They are gone," Yale hollered.

Altamont cut the rope attached to the hansom, and four men caught Johnson as his body dropped from the lamppost.

Chapter 1

Handing off information was the most dangerous part of his mission. However perilous, the updates were vital to Scotland Yard's investigation of the dastardly enemy he was monitoring. He was embedded with men who were extremely paranoid and not totally trustful of him. One thing was sure. The handoff had to be smooth and undetected.

No more than fifty yards away sat the bench where he would stash the information. However, less than twenty-five yards behind lurked a shadowy figure that had been following him for the past fifteen minutes. No doubt someone assigned to watch his every move.

There was no way he was going to leave this particular parcel while in full view of his stalker. He would have to cancel this drop. He pulled his pipe out and slowly packed it with tobacco. Upon lighting it, he began his stroll again. This was the signal to his contact that plans had changed. There would be no drop off this night.

He deliberately made the drops in the colored neighborhoods of Chicago. A person tailing him, especially a white man, would be far more detectable. The white man in the shadows came to a halt when the pipe was lit. It was clear he was the man following him. But how would he play this stroll off? And then he saw it. The newly opened restaurant he read about in the paper that was owned by a man who very much piqued his interest. He crossed the street and entered. He found a seat and picked up a magazine and began flipping through it. His stalker stopped across the street as if browsing inside a store looking at merchandise. The colored people walking the street gave him a strange inquiring look as they passed. He definitely was out of place. They knew it and he knew it. He soon disappeared.

The quiet little restaurant, Café de Champion sat humbly at the address of 41 W. 31st Street in an area of Chicago heavily populated by colored residents. It was August in the "Windy City," and the area had long since thawed from its chilling winter snows and given away to high temperatures.

However warm the weather in the city the atmosphere around it was desolate and cold bespeaking an uncertain future and fear.

Tragically, the *RMS Titanic* had sunk in April killing 1500 passengers and while more Britons died than Americans, the United States initiated an official inquiry into the *RMS Titanic* disaster, hastily issuing subpoenas for White Star personnel before they could return to the United Kingdom.

And though the country celebrated the openings of Tiger Stadium in Detroit, Michigan and Fenway Park in Boston, Massachusetts – which undoubtedly bolstered the quality of America's national pastime baseball – this was somewhat dampened due to growing rumors of an impending world-wide war rippling through the nation.

But for colored people of that day, a sinister shadow prevailed over the landscape, and nationally there unfurled something hideous and unprecedented. In 1911, there were sixty heinous acts of lynching of colored Americans, followed in 1912 by sixty-one more. Colored people in the United States were under siege and now lived in constant fear for their lives.

Nevertheless there was some cause for optimism. New

Jersey Governor and Democratic presidential candidate Woodrow Wilson was heavily favored to win the presidency that November, and many hoped present Republican President William Taft was on his way out. New Mexico had just been admitted as the forty-seventh state, signaling the growth of the nation. And within Café de Champion's humble confines, a meeting of historical proportions was unfolding.

The huge colored man moved hurriedly around his new restaurant. First he went to the kitchen for a check of food preparation, and the cooks and waiters all greeted him as if he were royalty. In a sense, among the colored race, he was. From there he ambled into the dining area to make a final inspection for cleanliness.

Then he noticed him. He had not seen him enter, but at a corner table with his back to the wall sat a singular white man. The colored man took particular note of how the gentleman had seated himself to assure he had an optimal view of every action that occurred in the tiny restaurant. Even more curiously, the white gentleman was reading intently the newest edition of the National Association for the Advancement of Colored People (NAACP) magazine called *The Crisis*. White folks in America looked upon the publication with disdain, but not this odd bird. He seemed genuinely interested in its contents.

Was this mysterious man a health inspector? Could he possibly be from the federal prosecutor's office? Perhaps he was one of those pesky, opportunistic reporters who hounded him for an exclusive story. Could this explain his interest in *The Crisis*? All these possibilities came to the colored man's mind as he surveyed the white gentleman. The list of folks trying to harass him of late was endless. Only one way to know for sure, he concluded as he made his way to the white man's table.

As the colored man approached he noticed the white man's distinguished-looking hawk-like facial features. The man's small beady eyes left the pages of *The Crisis* and darted throughout the restaurant, settling upon its owner. Twinkles of excitement seem to flicker in the white man's eyes as the colored man spoke to him.

"Welcome to Café de Champion," the colored man said as he extended his right arm to shake hands. The white man responded by placing *The Crisis* on the table and extending his arm to expose his small hand. The restaurant owner's gold tooth glittered from the light of dimly lit candles and his huge hand enveloped the smaller white hand. "And you are?"

"Altamont," said the man.

"What business brings you here, my fine friend?" asked the colored man.

"No business actually. I've heard about the opening of this fine establishment and thought I might venture here for a meal and exposure to a different cultural cuisine," Altamont said.

The colored man eyed Altamont curiously, wanting desperately to believe the man was at the Café de Champion for a meal-seeking, sightseeing excursion, but his experiences of late with white folk made him less trusting.

"Is that a British accent I detect?" asked the colored man.

"It is," Altamont replied. Because of the nature of the business that brought Altamont to America, and to Chicago expressly, he had learned to answer all questions laconically.

"Well, what do you think of my new restaurant?" continued the colored man. "Have you had a chance to sample Southern colored folk's cuisine? I may be starting the restaurant in the northern part of America, but the menu is purely Southern."

"Your place is enchanting," Altamont said. "And, no, I haven't had an opportunity to try the food of which you speak."

The colored man eyed Altamont and determined he meant him no harm, but there was something mysterious about him still. He didn't say much, that was certain, but for some reason the restaurant owner liked the mysterious white man and felt him to be a kindred spirit. "Then let me put together a special dish for you, and we can talk more," he said as he excused himself from the table and moved athletically into the kitchen. On a plate he heaped a huge serving of ham hocks and beside that the largest and most golden fried chicken breast he could find. He scooped a huge amount of cabbage, careful to sprinkle it liberally with vinegar, and finished the plate of food with candied yams.

While the colored man busied himself in the kitchen, Altamont scolded himself for his error. When England's premier and foreign minister had approached him in London to come out of retirement to bring down a particularly dangerous Irish spy ring one of his concerns was the possible decline in his usually keen intellect due to age. When the black man asked if his accent was British, he had said yes. His undercover identity was as an Irishman. In the wrong company such a blunder could have meant instant death. He made a mental note to be more careful in the upcoming verbal exchange.

As Altamont, he had to maintain the guise of a bitter Irishman in order to gain any success in his mission. Admitting to an English accent was a major blunder.

The colored man suddenly re-appeared at the table, plate in hand.

"Will that be enough?" he asked, chest protruded, knowing a "no" was out of the question.

"More than enough," replied Altamont. He sampled a morsel of each item and followed each tasting with an analytical conclusion of "umm."

A huge smile spread across the colored man's face as Altamont graciously yet speedily consumed his meal. It was obvious the mysterious white man had been so engrossed in the business that brought him to America that eating had not been a priority.

As Altamont neared the end of his meal he sat back and pushed his near empty plate forward.

"Mr. Johnson," Altamont said, "the meal is exquisite, but I'm afraid you have simply given me too much to consume."

Jack Johnson's huge right hand reached over, lifted the plate and moved it away from Altamont.

"Then you do know who I am," said Jack Johnson, looking directly into Altamont's beady eyes.

"You are Jack Johnson, America's first Negro heavyweight boxing champion. Furthermore, you are the most feared and yet most controversial champion ever," Altamont informed him. "I, in my more youthful folly fancied myself a competitive pugilist, but my skill level was never to the caliber of yours, I'm afraid."

"The fear and controversy are one and the same from where I sit," Johnson said with a weary sadness.

"And though many fear your boxing prowess, you sir, have your own fear," Altamont said. "Why won't you put your heavyweight title on the line against fighters of your race? Why fight only white men?"

Johnson found himself on verbal defense and somewhat surprised. Altamont was embarking on a subject Johnson traditionally refused to address.

Altamont had him pegged. Johnson refused to fight dangerous colored fight challengers like Sam Langford, Joe Jeannette, and Sam McVey. All three colored fighters were more than capable of taking his coveted title, a title Johnson cherished, a title he wasn't in a hurry to relinquish.

Altamont pressed on. "It would seem to me with your having broken the color barrier you would be more than willing to make the heavyweight title available to all races, but I'm sure you have your reasons as to why not."

At the same time Altamont could only deduce the sources of prejudice that contributed to the sadness in Johnson's voice as he responded to how the world perceived him. Before him sat a colored man who verbally taunted white men in the boxing ring while physically pummeling them into submission with his huge black fists. If that wasn't insult enough to a white American society that viewed themselves superior to their colored counterparts, then Johnson sealed the deal for their hatred of him by not just openly sleeping with white women, but also having the audacity to marry them. He also exhibited the seemingly hypocritical position of shutting out other colored fighters from a title bout, more than likely providing cause for some whiplash and snide comments from those within Johnson's race. Johnson was indeed in a dubious position.

"Perhaps it was your destiny to be a heavyweight champion," Altamont said, "but it's was your choice to consort with white women. You know such a practice in America is taboo, at least, it being practiced for all of white America to see. You had to know there would be repercussions."

Altamont was aware that native Africans were kidnapped or sold to white slave traffickers by rival tribes and then transported to America to become the backbone of the country's labor force, a labor force that received no compensation. They survived the ordeal until Abraham Lincoln signed into law the "Emancipation Proclamation." And still, the colored Americans were treated as second-class citizens. But Johnson, by the might of his fists, had circumvented his submission to the caste system white America was trying to forge.

"You are anomalous," Altamont told Johnson.

"What does anomalous mean, Altamont?" Johnson asked. "I'm not sure if you're aware of this or not, but I only completed five years of formal schooling. When white folks use big words like that I try to learn them."

Altamont smiled. Despite the limited educational background Johnson had secured, it was obvious his intellect was keen. "To be anomalous, Mr. Johnson, means, in essence, you simply should not exist. No colored man should be doing what you do in this particular era. I'm confident that as this American society evolves, relations between colored and white people will advance, and consorting between white women and colored men will become commonplace. In essence, what you desire to do and are presently doing is at best a half century before it's time."

Johnson stared down at the table and seemed introspective. "Altamont that makes sense and perhaps explains why there were race riots in 1910 when I beat James J. Jeffries in Reno, Nevada. Boy, white folks had billed our match as the fight of the century. They were convinced this big white boy would beat me senseless and perhaps back to reality. Did you know that novelist Jack London wrote in a New York newspaper that it was a match 'between a colossus and a pygmy. Burns was a toy in his hands. Jim Jeffries must emerge from his alfalfa farm and remove the golden smile from Johnson's face. Jeff, it's up to you.' Their first in a list of 'Great White Hopes' that were and will be sent against me, I'm sure."

"The riots no doubt were repercussions of an enraged white society that failed in putting you and your arrogance in its place," Altamont said. "They were in shock and horror because you, a singular colored man, were tearing down the walls of an American system that white people saw as galvanized and impregnable to the accomplishment you were achieving," Altamont said with a smile.

Johnson concurred with Altamont's summation.

"Boy, you're telling me," Johnson said. "I beat Burns in Sydney, Australia in 1908 for the heavyweight title, but the shock of my win was so devastating that it took the white folks until 1910 to officially award it to me."

Both Altamont and Johnson burst out in laughter with that said, clearly releasing the tension built up by the subject matter.

Johnson was impressed by Altamont's introspect of his situation, but he was no longer in the mood to talk about the prejudicial world in which he evolved.

"Are you a man of the arts, Mr. Altamont?" Johnson inquired. "I have an extra ticket to my favorite opera 'II Trovatore' that starts in less than an hour."

Altamont thought this invitation to be a perfect opportunity. The trail of his mission had gone cold for the moment, and attending the famous opera would be good for his cover. He would be perceived as just an average Irishman taking in a cultural event while touring North America. "I'd love to go," he said.

Within minutes Altamont found himself in the passenger seat of one of Johnson's famous roadsters. Johnson reached speeds well above the legal limits posted on road signs. Altamont tried desperately to contain the exasperation on his face while holding on to his American styled Stetson.

"One day, I'll probably die in one of these babies," Johnson said as he motored into fourth gear, causing the engine to roar furiously as Altamont's head snapped backwards.

Altamont silently concurred as the wind blasted his hawkish face. Altamont wondered if this was in some way a confession by Johnson of how he wanted to die. Did he want to die as he lived, under his own terms and within his own passion?

As the two men stood outside the theatre, Johnson displayed a vulnerability that perhaps he had never showed to any other of the white race. Altamont was honored. "I'm scared, Altamont," he said, unable to make eye contact. "Since white men cannot beat me in the ring, they have chosen to criminalize me. In June of this year I was indicted for smuggling a diamond into the country. Had a white man done this, the infraction would probably have been minimized and he would be shielded from the press, but I was castigated by the white media."

"Chin up, old boy," Altamont said with a chuckle. "The best is yet to come from what I understand. It seems there are reports of your being arrested soon for violating the 'White Slavery Traffic Act,' and that, my dear chap, could truly be your undoing."

"I should be angered by your chuckle, but the 'Mann Act,' also known as the White Slavery Act of which they have charged me is laughable, I agree," Johnson returned. "I took a white woman I was involved with across a state line, and the fact I plan on marrying her had no bearing. My attorney says what they want to prosecute me for is an intentional misuse of the Mann Act. The law was intended to halt the interstate trafficking of prostitutes, so in essence they are accusing me of being a pimp. I assure you, Altamont, my woman is my woman, and I'm not in the business of sharing or selling her."

There was no more said in regards to Johnson's criminalization. They both shared the wonderment of 'Il Trovatore,' and throughout the performance Altamont would look at Johnson who sat next to him, eyes closed as if to soak in every sound. This brute of a colored man was now docile, immersed in the reverie of his passion for the arts. Altamont admired the anomalous man beside him.

Outside the theatre, the men bade farewell. "Sure you won't let me drop you at home?" Johnson asked. He smiled as

Altamont motioned no with his palms thrust outward. Johnson knew after his first ride to the theatre he could bet on Altamont's saying no.

"One question, Altamont. Do you know the great detective Sherlock Holmes? Your being from Europe and all, I wonder if you ever met him?" Johnson asked.

"I know him well," Altamont said casually.

"I hear that the hate for Mr. Holmes by criminals in England is much like that of what I experience with white folks here in America. It figures you know him what you call 'well,' Altamont. He, from what I hear, shares the same loves as you and I," Johnson said while eyeing Altamont for a flicker of emotion. "He too is a pugilist, arts enthusiast, has beady eyes and a hawk-like face much like yours, Altamont. They say he is a master of disguises and that he will sometimes put a bust in front of his room's window in case a sniper is lurking." Johnson turned to walk in the direction of his car.

"Perhaps you will meet him if you ever make it to England," Altamont said.

"I have to," Johnson said. "I could be wrong but he, like me and you, is an anomalous character in his own right."

" Mr. Johnson, if someone should inquire of you as to what we discussed please, for the sake of my safety, say that I am Irish," Altamont said, hoping to cover his tracks.

"Altamont, you're so Irish when I look at you, all I see is green," Johnson quipped. "You know we anomalous folks must look out for one another."

Johnson waved his hand and disappeared into the darkness.

Altamont melted in the darkness as well.

Chapter 2

Two days passed, and as Jack Johnson busied himself in the kitchen of Café de Champion, he found himself wondering who this Altamont was, where he was and what sort of company he kept. There was a mysterious aura surrounding the man's demeanor, though not one where evil lurks. No, this man had a good spirit. And having been in his company was far more refreshing than the company of any white man Johnson had ever encountered.

As Johnson exited the kitchen, he saw Altamont sitting at the table where they first met. Seated next to him was another white man, a rather curious looking man with a sly look and a face that brought Johnson to immediate distrust. Johnson approached the table, shook Altamont's hand enthusiastically, and then took a seat beside him while eyeing carefully the man who sat with Altamont.

"Welcome back to the Café de Champion, Altamont, my Irish friend," Johnson said. He saw the happiness in Altamont's face that his return was welcomed and that he had been referred to as Irish. "And you are?"

The white man seated beside Altamont shook Johnson's hand. "Let's just say I'm a 'friend' of Altamont's."

"Well, despite the fact you have no name, any friend of Altamont is a friend of mine," Johnson said coyly. Upon saying that, he excused himself from the table and exited into the kitchen, returning minutes later. A thuggish looking colored man entered the dining area through the kitchen seconds after Johnson. Johnson pointed to an area outside the café where diners could eat, telling him to wait at a table there.

"This is very awkward for me Mr. Johnson," Altamont said. "I assure you that my initial visit was purely fortuitous, and I had no agenda. However, my friend here became aware of our friendship. It appears he and a few of his friends have invested in an Irish-American boxer here in Chicago and they want to see where he is in his development."

Johnson gave Altamont a knowing smile. "I see, and perhaps the best way for them to gauge this boxer is to pair him against me?"

"Exactly, Mr. Johnson, an exhibition, non-title fight, and we will pay you quite handsomely for your participation. There will be a private audience in attendance, men and women who will pay well to witness the event," said Altamont's friend. "We're raising funds for a good cause, which I have no liberty to speak about at the moment."

"Good cause, I bet," Johnson whispered under his breath.

Then Altamont spoke. "Now, Mr. Johnson, if you see this request as a violation of our friendship, I and my friend will leave immediately."

"Quite the contrary, Altamont. We anomalous types have to look after one another," Johnson said. " Set the match for eight p.m. this evening, and tell your Irish-American stable boy to be prepared to fight a 20-round exhibition match, and I will not hold back just because he's someone's investment. Now tell me, how handsome is my pay in this?"

Altamont's friend removed a wrapped stack of crisp American one hundred dollar bills, and after making his count, Johnson whistled. "I tell you one thing Altamont, you sure know how to put money in a colored fellow's pocket," Johnson smiled, gold tooth glinting in the light.

Altamont's friend handed Johnson a slip of paper with the address of the event on it. The friend seemed excited, walking ahead of Johnson and Altamont as they stepped outside the restaurant.

"One moment, gentlemen," Johnson said, walking toward the colored man who had been sitting quietly outside the restaurant at a table near the entrance. Johnson saw Altamont look into the man's eyes. Like Altamont, when Johnson looked into the man's eyes, they held a cold, still glaze within. The man had the eyes of death; he was an assassin, and Johnson hoped Altamont would not notice. After whispering into the man's ear and the thuggish looking man disappeared into the shadows.

"Would you excuse us for a moment, sir? I need to have a word with Mr. Johnson," Altamont told his friend, and he and Johnson walked a few feet away. When Altamont was sure his friend could not hear him, he spoke. "I'm sorry, Mr. Johnson, that I mixed you up in my sordid affair. I think it was unfair for my Irish friend to ask you to fight tonight. I suspected my friend had someone follow me the other night. Make no mistake, sir, we are affiliated with a dangerous group of Irish snakes."

"No worse than the white American snakes I deal with every day," Johnson retorted. "Besides, the years have taught me well how to cover my back. See you at eight, Altamont."

Altamont walked away comforted that Johnson knew how to cover his back. Altamont vaguely heard his friend chattering to him excitedly about the night's upcoming fight. Altamont agreed, however, with his friend, it would indeed be an interesting affair.

Darkness descended upon the city of Chicago as Johnson's roadster roared to an abrupt stop in front of an abandoned warehouse on Chicago's Southside. The area was controlled by a local gang called the "Chicago Outfit," and many a person had disappeared in this dangerous part of the city.

Johnson got out, surveyed the area, and smiled. This was perfect for him and the "special guests" he had invited to the fight. Three cars filled with men in dark suits were parked across the street in the shadows. Johnson held his left hand up with all five fingers extended to indicate they should enter in five minutes. Just then, Altamont stepped from the shadow of the warehouse and greeted Johnson. Altamont's face was somber.

"An informant loyal to me within my friend's organization told me that the friend we're involved with will have me led away midway through your fight," Altamont told Johnson. "It appears the group will hold me hostage in hope of forcing you to sign a contract allowing them to serve as your fight agents."

"Oh, there will be some bargaining all right, but they won't be doing it," Johnson said in a cavalier tone. "Relax, Altamont, this isn't my first rodeo with these types of people. Where's the boxing ring?"

Altamont and Johnson entered the makeshift boxing arena. There were people everywhere, all well-dressed and apparently well-heeled, as they sported diamonds and gold on various parts of their bodies. A particularly attractive white woman, a sumptuously shapely blonde, caught Johnson's eye, and he blew her a kiss while winking at her. One white gentleman approached Altamont asking in an Irish accent if he had seen their friend since the meeting at the Café de Champion. It was only then that Altamont noticed the friend was not in the building.

Unbeknownst to Altamont, Johnson had Altamont's friend followed and kidnapped by the mysterious colored man who had waited patiently outside the café had, upon Johnson's order, followed and kidnapped Altamont's Irish friend. Johnson believed that since the man had been so brash as to come to his restaurant and refuse to give his name, he had to be up to no good. By holding the friend hostage Johnson now had the upper hand.

"I have the arrogant snob," Johnson said as he grabbed the much smaller inquisitor by the collar and lifted him from the earth. "Go. Tell your cohorts he will not be returned until I finish my boxing match. How dare him come to my turf, my restaurant, and not tell me his name. I tire of white folks and their games, and he pissed me off this afternoon with his disrespect. I'm not taking it from someone who is alien to this country. Altamont and I will be far away from this place when you see your friend again. Go tell your Irish buddies what I said."

The expressions of the friend's associates were first those of gloom and disbelief, turning quickly to shadows of hate. They were beaten, their plan to abduct Altamont checkmated. It got worse.

But to Altamont, the conversation Johnson had with the

mysterious colored man outside the restaurant earlier that day now was evident. Johnson had the man tail his friend and kidnap him. Despite Johnson's limited education, Altamont came to understand that Johnson was as intelligent as any man he had crossed paths with, perhaps just as devious too.

Johnson grabbed one of the Irishmen designated as a sentry, slapped him across his face, and grabbed him by the neck, forcing him to open the door leading into the warehouse before anyone could react. Within seconds, ten white men in suits and fedoras came rushing in, armed to the teeth with Tommy-guns and pistols. Seconds later, a large white man entered. He wore a white suit, a diamond pin in his silk tie, and a diamond ring. The man who walked in behind him seemed to be in command of the ten mobsters who flashed their weapons brazenly. The distinguished looking man in the white suit took a seat next to the door near the boxing ring.

"My personal security team," bellowed Johnson as the white men stationed themselves strategically throughout the small arena. None showed emotion in their faces. Johnson made his way to the ring, climbed through the ropes, and began calling loudly for his opponent. Johnson had removed his overcoat and dress slacks to reveal his bare chest and boxing trunks. Johnson reached for his boxing gloves that he had brought with him.

"Come to the center of the ring, and let's get started," Johnson said to his Irish-American opponent, beckoning him to the ring as he tugged on his personal boxing gloves. The redheaded kid looked barely 21-years-old, but he was tall and wide with cannon-sized biceps. His face showed fear, and Johnson could smell it. Johnson taunted him because of it.

"Which one of your white Irish buddies did you make so mad that he wanted to punish you by putting you in the ring with me?" Johnson jeered as the bell for the first round sounded. He flashed his usual big smile, allowing the light to glisten off of his golden tooth.

The redhead moved into the ring cautiously. Anyone in the makeshift arena could see in his eyes that he didn't like what Johnson had said to him, and he wanted to knock Johnson's head off. For the first five rounds he tried desperately to do just that, unloading powerful roundhouse punches that found only air where Johnson's head had microseconds before been previously exposed. The redhead had not done his homework, Altamont thought to himself. This was vintage Johnson boxing style, fighting cautiously early in the fight and then becoming more aggressive as the fight continued. By the eleventh round, the redhead's left eye was bleeding profusely from Johnson's powerful right-hand punches while his right eye was so swollen from Johnson's counterpunches he could barely see. Blood had begun to trickle from the corner of his mouth, the result of a loosened tooth. Sadly, the audience knew Johnson was actually holding back from really doing serious damage. By the eighteenth round, the redhead's corner threw in the towel. Their boy refused to answer the bell.

Johnson jumped out of the ring, seemingly not having exerted much effort, and walked to the group of investors.

"Your boy needs some more fights before he's ready. And for the record, Altamont is under my protection. If anything happens to him, you won't see me, but I assure you that you will not see the light of the next day. And tell your friend that after I release him he's not to visit me again unless he provides a name. That's why I had my folks grab him. He needs to learn to be more respectful." With that Johnson and Altamont made their way to the door.

Then Johnson spun on his heels turning around as if remembering something. He pointed to the corner, at the Irishman who had asked about the absence of Altamont's friend. He waved the man over and spoke once the man stood in front of him. It was apparent in the man's face he that was suffering from a high degree of fear.

"I am so rude my dear Irish friend. I invited this gentleman in the finely tailored white suit and sparkling diamonds to the fight because he was so kind as to allow his associates to serve as my personal security team. Let me introduce him," Johnson said as he placed his right hand on the frightened man's shoulder while pointing with his left index finger. "His name is "Diamond Jim" Colosimo, and nothing goes on in this town without his knowing. The guy beside him, I only know as 'The Fox' Torrio"

The Irish man's facial features dropped into an expression of gloom at the mention of the name "Diamond Jim."

Altamont knew all too well who "Diamond Jim" Colosimo was. Colosimo was the leader of an organized crime syndicate in Chicago called the "Chicago Outfit." The Outfit had built quite a lucrative financial empire for Colosimo through his criminal ventures of prostitution, gambling and racketeering. Colosimo was a key player in what American law enforcement called "The Mafia."

The man beside him was John "The Fox" Torrio. Torrio

was Colosimo's cousin. He came to Chicago from Brooklyn, New York in 1909 to be Colosimo's second-in-command when a rival gang called the "Black Hand" started to become a threat. Unlike the New York crime syndicate that had five controlling crime families that were governed by what was called "The Commission," in Chicago there were very few rivals for Colosimo, and he maintained virtual control of the city's underworld single-handedly. Torrio was Colosimo's "muscle" within the organization.

It was Torrio who stepped forward to the Irishman as Johnson stepped away to make room. There was a confident gaze in Torrio's eyes as he looked the frightened Irishman up and down, from head to toe.

"My Irish friend, what is your name?" Torrio asked.

"Shane," the frightened Irishman replied.

"Well Shane, my boss, Mr. Colosimo was extremely upset when he heard a gang of Irish immigrants had set up shop in his city," Torrio said coolly.

Shane shook his head.

"No sir," Shane said. "We haven't set up shop, and we certainly aren't a gang."

"What? Am I stupid here?" Torrio bellowed, as he pointed at all the Irishmen who were excused from security duty when he and his crew entered the building. Some of the spectators sitting at the makeshift ringside seats shifted in their chairs feeling ill at ease with the revelation of who was in their midst.

"I bet these folks paid a pretty sum to see the famous Jack Johnson fight. And since this is a part of the city of

Chicago and since Mr. Colosimo manages all Chicago, I think it only fair he shares in the proceeds. Let's see, since you never asked permission to hold this event, I'd say seventy-five percent of what you earned from these folks should be fair compensation. Who has your cash box?" Torrio raised his right fist in the air, and his ten mobster henchmen raised their weapons, at the ready to shoot.

Shane expelled a sigh of resignation as he motioned for the cashier to bring him the cash box.

"Well, I can see you boys are conducting business, so let me get out of your way," Johnson said with a devilish smile as he slapped the Irishman on his back, forcing him to lunge forward. He grabbed Altamont by the elbow and began ushering him to the door when Diamond Jim motioned for Johnson to come his direction. He peeled away five crisp one hundred dollar bills from a wad of cash.

"Thank you, Jack, for letting us know that such a travesty was taking place right under our noses without our knowledge until you told us. Obviously the gentlemen don't understand the rules of this city. Nothing like this happens unless I get a slice of the pie," Colosimo said as he slipped the cash into Johnson's moist hand. "We will correct this problem immediately."

"Don't mention it Diamond Jim," Johnson said with a chuckle.

"I would like for you – and what's his name?" asked Diamond Jim.

"Altamont, and no finer man of his race have I met," Johnson said. "Present company excluded, I might add."

"I would like you and Altamont to visit me at Colosimo's Café in an hour for dinner," Colosimo said. "I'll have the boys keep everyone inside so you won't be followed or retaliated against, and I will let these fine Irishmen know you and Altamont are under my protection. That should keep you safe."

Johnson noticed Altamont chuckling to himself. The anomalous Johnson knew why. In this case, as in many others, Johnson had his way with white folks, setting the rules and telling them the way things were going to be. And they paid him good money to do it. Altamont was getting a first-hand look at why white America hated Johnson.

"I suppose the boxing world in which you evolve exposes you to such unsavory characters as Diamond Jim and Torrio," Altamont said.

"You shouldn't be so judgmental, Altamont," Johnson said. "That group of Irish rattlesnakes we left back at the warehouse was not the sort of men a woman would take home to meet her family. Just what is it you do, Altamont, if I might ask?"

Altamont smiled. His country's mission was taking a toll on him. In his early years, being in the presence of such rascals went against every sensibility he had but he did so for the sake of his investigations. Tonight seemed like no exception. He found himself admiring Diamond Jim's power and Torrio's propensity to strike fear into the hearts of men. The fact Colosimo and Torrio invoked fear into the hearts of the dangerous Irish criminals he was now consorting with seemed paradoxical since these same Irish thugs had invoked similar fear into the hearts of their adversaries. Even more alarming was his excitement at being invited to dine with Diamond Jim. Altamont was thinking it was his advancing age that had dulled his sensitivities a bit, or after spending years dealing with some of the top European criminal masterminds, perhaps he wanted to understand the ways of American crime figures. One thing was sure, no matter the origin of the criminals or their crimes, they were capable of murder if they felt they were betrayed or felt they were being spied on. Altamont had to stay on top of his game or surely a dagger would one day pierce his heart, a bullet hit a vital organ or his air cut off by hands adept at using a garrotte cutting off his breathing.

"Mr. Johnson, I truly am not at liberty to say what it is I do, but it is perilous and stressful," Altamont said. "I will say being in your company is a welcome diversion, and I thrill at the fact that I have no idea what you will do next or are capable of doing. I do know there is a great deal of good in you, and yet you place yourself in the most controversial circumstances in the society in which you live."

"Fair enough, Altamont. You have avoided answering my question, so I shall never ask again," Johnson said.

The hour passed swiftly, and Altamont found himself seated at the table with some of Chicago's top criminals and killers. The unsettling part of the scenario was that, because of Diamond Jim's pronouncement that he would tell the Irishmen he and Johnson were under his protection, Altamont was in league with them. While taking no personal comfort in this, this situation could play in his favor. The Irishmen would fear him because of his association with The Outfit, and this could give him value and leverage in his dealings.

At the head of the table, of course, sat Diamond Jim, and alongside him, his wife Victoria. To his right his trusted muscle man John "The Fox" Torrio. To Colosimo's left sat two of Chicago's top politicians, saloonkeeper Michael "Hinky Dink" Kenna and a bathhouse owner named "Bathhouse" John Coughlin. Altamont was seated with Hinky Dink and Bathhouse three chairs down, while Johnson sat directly across from Altamont beside Torrio.

Colosimo started his criminal empire working as a pimp. At the same time he also had a legitimate job with Chicago's street-sweepers. He soon rose to the rank of foreman, which is not surprising, since the street-sweepers were almost exclusively Italian, and he was one of the rare few who could speak English. He also organized a social and athletic club for his workmates, and naturally much of the profits found their way into his pocket. With his job, the club, and his women, he earned enough money to open a pool hall in the First Ward. Through his prostitution racket, he gained a reputation as a tough criminal and attracted the attention of the Democrat Party. Altamont was intrigued: politicians in bed with known criminals?

Hinky Dink and Bathhouse were the aldermen for the First Ward and Democrats. As aldermen, Kenna and Coughlin had a lot of political clout in Chicago and consequently used that control to make money from the city's brothels. They hired Diamond Jim to collect protection money from the city's pimps. Those who paid felt secure in the fact that their businesses would remain untouched by the police. Those who didn't pay found their insolence met with violence.

One brothel madam who had bought this protection was his wife, seated next to him, Victoria Moresco, a woman who fell in love with Big Jim. The two were married in 1902. By then, Colosimo owned a pool hall, a saloon, and now his wife's bordello, and, combined with his share of the generous financial gains by providing protection for the Democrats, he was fast becoming a wealthy man. He and Victoria opened many more prostitution dens and muscled in on the businesses of other pimps. At the height of his power, Big Jim owned or shared in the profits of an estimated 200 whorehouses.

Prostitution was a booming industry in the Levee district, and supply was far outweighed by demand. Chicago needed a new source of hookers, so, with another married couple, Maurice and Julia Van Bever, the Colosimos set up Chicago's White Slave Ring. The slavers kidnapped young girls, beat and raped them into submission and sold them to pimps for $400 each. They specifically targeted immigrant girls who could not speak English, making it more difficult for the girls to get help. Many of their victims were underage teenagers who were easier to control and more popular with the customers. Most of these girls were sold to slavers in other states so that it would be more difficult for their families to track them down. The Colosimos and Van Bevers also supplied local pimps with girls kidnapped from cities out-of-state. The White Slave Ring had contacts in Kansas City, St. Louis, Milwaukee, and New York.

On the way to Colosimo's Café, Johnson had filled Altamont in on Colosimo's and his associates' past, and Altamont was grateful for this information. Altamont was saddened, however, that as he viewed all the folks at the table he couldn't distinguish who the real criminals were, the gangsters or the politicians. One thing was clear, they seemed to be one happy family.

Diamond Jim's face sported a distinguished nose perched atop a bushy, full moustache. His demeanor carried the air of power, as did his voice.

"Bathhouse, sorry about the mess in taking care of that business with that pimp down by the docks," Diamond Jim said. "I think he should be released from the hospital real soon. Hate it when things get to that point."

Bathhouse Coughlin seemed hesitant to acknowledge Diamond Jim at first. He cast an uncomfortable glance in the direction of Altamont.

"Jack and his friend Altamont are fine. They're with me. You can speak freely," Diamond Jim said.

"You did what you had to do, Diamond Jim, I don't fault you for that," Bathhouse replied. "Force is the only thing some of those low-life pimps understand. You got my money, right?"

"Oh yeah, that little whore he calls his woman went to the spot where he hid the cash and paid us just so we didn't kill him," Diamond Jim said with a chuckle. "I made her give me a bit more for pissing me off, in fact."

There was a chuckle exchanged around the table.

Hinky Dink Kenna chimed in. "We're going to need some new girls soon. I'm getting sick of a few of those whores who have too much mouth. We beat them but it doesn't seem to help. I think we'll have to close their eyes and send a message to the other girls."

"Before you do that, give them to me," Victoria said,

offering a solution. "Sometimes it just takes a woman's touch to get that type of woman in line. I can handle them."

Hinky Dink nodded, agreeing to turn the troublesome prostitutes over to Victoria. He really didn't want to kill them, but would if there were no other options. Of course he would want financial compensation to unload them to Victoria.

The conversation hushed as the waiter poured some red wine around the table.

"The Van Devers sent me a message saying they're bringing some young runaways from St. Louis within the next few days," Diamond Jim said. "I'll have some of my boys break them in and get them over to you."

"As long as it's your boys doing the breaking in and not you my dear Mr. Colosimo," Victoria said with an air of jealousy. She loved Diamond Jim and resented the fact that he would take up with a new prostitute who caught his fancy from time to time.

"Not here, Victoria. You know this is my business, and I was doing this when we met," Diamond Jim said. "Don't make me knock the crap out of you."

Johnson broke the tense air created. "I'm hungry, Diamond Jim, but not for food at this moment. Is that red-head Flo over at the Double Deuce still?"

"I thought you might ask about her, so I had her not take any customers in case you wanted to see her," said Victoria, ever the businesswoman. "She sure has taken a shine to you."

"I'm not sure if it's me Flo takes a shine to or if it's the extra money I pay her. Could be both," Johnson said sarcastically. "Altamont, I'm going to take a stroll over to the

Double Deuce. Care to join me? I'll treat you as well."

"I'll pass," Altamont said, somewhat repulsed by the suggestion.

"We'll take care of you, Altamont," Diamond Jim said. "Jack, you go and have a good time with Flo. We'll get Altamont a cab and get him home safely."

Johnson winked at Altamont and made his way to the door.

Altamont was not fooled one bit. Diamond Jim wanted him to stay so he could get to the bottom of who Altamont was and determine the nature of his business in Chicago. As Johnson disappeared, Diamond Jim wasted little time. "Well, Altamont, Jack seems to really like you. He doesn't let too many people into his inner circle, so I'm impressed. He sure seemed to save your bacon at that warehouse when the Irishmen wanted to kidnap you? What's your business here in Chicago, and why are you running with that rag-tag group of Irishmen?"

Every eye at the table was focused on Altamont, awaiting his response.

"With all due respect, Mr. Colosimo, I really am not at liberty to talk about my particular business here in Chicago," Altamont said, careful to use a respectful tone. "I can assure you what I do here has absolutely no bearing on what you do here in Chicago, and I plan on heading out to Buffalo, New York within the next few days. I pose no threat to you"

Again there was silence, and stares still focused on him.

"To be honest, I have no idea what you do except that Mr. Johnson says you are a very shrewd businessman. I'm happy with that knowledge, and out of mutual courtesy, please accept that I am just simply honored to be in the presence of such distinguished gentlemen."

The men around the table looked at each other and then burst into laughter.

"I hope you're using that term gentlemen very loosely," Victoria said as the men still maintained their laughter.

"Very, very loosely," Hinky Dink said, doubling over with laughter at this point.

"He's not from Chicago, that's for sure," Bathhouse said regaining his composure.

"You don't have to suck up to us, Altamont," Diamond Jim said with a smile on his face. "If I didn't trust you, I would have had you killed the moment Jack walked out the door. Eat my friend."

The waiter placed the food on the table, and the criminals and politicians began eating heartily. But as Altamont consumed his spaghetti and meatballs, he made occasional glances at The Fox. In Torrio's eyes he saw the same shadows of death he saw in the eyes of the colored man Johnson had hired to abduct Altamont's friend. No doubt Torrio was a killer, and Altamont observed him to be a man of little loyalty if it came down to getting what he wanted. As a teenager, John became an important member of the New York based Five Points Gang, one of the cities largest and most powerful gangs. He was also the head of an affiliated gang, The James Street Gang. He was known by his peers as Terrible Johnny in his early years and lived up to his nickname on various occasions when rival gangs clashed with his own. He was looked upon as cold, cruel, and calculating. He was short but tough and had a natural flair as a violent man, so violent a reputation he was asked to be bouncer at one of the toughest bars in Manhattan at that time, Nigger Mike's Pub on Pell Street. In 1912, Torrio moved his attention to the bars and brothels in the dockyard areas of Brooklyn. Every now and then, he would offer employment to his fellow James Street Gang members. Each of his exploits fed his dream of organizing crime into a big business. As early as 1909, Torrio was traveling to and from Chicago to do business for his uncle Diamond Jim. Colosimo had some trouble with extortionists trying to take a vested interest in his profits. Torrio was asked to persuade them to go away. Several bloody corpses later, the word on the street was to leave Diamond Jim's prostitution business alone, or else.

  The Fox Torrio midway through the meal turned his attention to Altamont.

  "Altamont, you seem like a decent enough guy, so I'll shoot straight with you," Torrio said. "If we find out you are encroaching on any of our business here in Chicago, I'll kill you personally. No offense of course."

  Altamont looked across the table at Bathhouse, and without batting an eyelash said "pass the bread please." Once he took a slice he calmly spoke.

  "I'll be in Buffalo in a few days, so the chance of you extinguishing my life is minimal if non-existent," Altamont said as he chewed on his bread and smiled at Torrio.

  The look Torrio gave him brought Altamont inward amusement. He had answered coolly, without fear. Torrio didn't say it, but this garnered Altamont some respect with the killer. This was one rare occasion Torrio had not struck fear into a man's heart and he recognized that fact.

"You're a cool customer Altamont. I like that about you," Torrio said as he resumed eating. For Altamont, though, he knew just because Torrio liked an aspect of his character, the little tough guy would kill him at a moment's notice.

"Lighten up, fellows. No one is going to give anyone a reason to kill anyone. I believe Altamont is no threat, so let's leave it at that," Diamond Jim said.

Soon after the meal, Altamont stood.

"Mr. Colosimo, I cannot thank you enough for the hospitality you have shown me," Altamont said as he stood and gathered his coat and hat. "I wish you all luck in your future endeavors."

Diamond Jim wrote something on his business card and handed it to Altamont. The card contained his name and a number. The handwritten message read, "If you hurt or kill this man you will have to answer to Diamond Jim Colosimo, and I won't be in a good mood when I answer you."

"If any of those Irish pricks try to hurt you, hand them this and ask them to call me before they do anything," Colosimo said. Then he had two of his men return Altamont to his apartment across the city.

Altamont's friend and two of his Irish thugs appeared at Altamont's door minutes after he walked in.

"Why shouldn't I have you killed right here, right now for having me abducted?" the friend asked. Altamont coolly handed him Diamond Jim's card. The friend became silent.

"That card plus the fact it was Jack Johnson who had you abducted. I didn't find out until I entered the warehouse for the fight and you weren't there," Altamont said, looking the friend directly in the eyes. "I believe Diamond Jim will make good on what you just read. In fact he assured me of this while we shared dinner tonight so exercise wisdom in whatever decision you make. But if you decide not to kill me, I must ask you and your cohorts to leave and allow me to get some sleep. It has been a long day."

Altamont's friend sat for a moment overwhelmed by the reality he now faced in dealing with Altamont. Altamont could no longer be viewed or treated as some low level pawn in his plans, and with Altamont's obvious connection with the Chicago crime family, he could prove to be a far more valuable asset than ever envisioned.

"I realize you're tired Altamont, but first accept my apology for not trusting you," the friend said. "And your role in the trip to Buffalo has changed as well. You're a much more capable man than I realized, and I can give you far more responsibility."

"And the other apology you owe me, is that forthcoming?" Altamont asked. "The ill-fated plan you had to kidnap me in hopes of forcing Jack Johnson to let you manage him."

"For that I will apologize as well," the friend said.

Just at that moment there was a knock at the door. Altamont nodded his head for one of thugs to open it. The Fox Torrio walked in with two of his henchmen.

"Altamont, Mr. Colosimo asked me to come by and check on you to make sure our Irish friends didn't do anything to you," Torrio said as he eyed the three Irishmen. "You okay?"

"Fine," Altamont said. "The gentlemen were just leaving so I can get some sleep."

"We'll walk out with them," Torrio said opening the door and beckoning with his head for the Irishmen to walk out. They did. And Torrio left behind them only taking a moment to stick his head back in to wink at Altamont. While perhaps Colosimo had asked Torrio to make sure Altamont was safe against retaliation, his appearance was Torrio's way of letting Altamont know they knew where he lived.

Days later, Johnson received a carrier delivered note from Altamont. Altamont was in route to Buffalo and then Ireland.

To the Anomalous Mr. Johnson:

Our newly formed friendship has been the highlight of my stay in America. But my purpose for the trip has been intensified and I must now move on to Buffalo, New York and then Ireland.

If you should ever come to Europe, I am totally at your service.

I'll probably find you before you find me so until then Mr. Johnson.

Altamont

Johnson smiled, pulled out a book of matches, and burned the note.

Chapter 3

Jack Johnson's roadster exceeded the speed limit as it roared down the street to the Chicago dry-docks and came to an abrupt halt. Before exiting his car he simply leaned back and recounted his conversation with Altamont in the summer of 1912. He missed Altamont and remembered vividly Altamont's prediction that white America would convict him under the Mann Act.* Johnson should have felt privileged that American law makers had devised a law specifically for him, specifically to convict him, specifically to punish him for being what Altamont called "anomalous." But he didn't feel privileged; he felt singled out and persecuted. His passion for white women had enraged white men so deeply that it had driven them to this point.

He remembers the glee on the faces of the white police officers on October 18, 1912 as they hooked the steel handcuffs to his wrist and announced proudly he was being arrested for violating the Mann Act. The arrest was made on the grounds that his relationship with Lucille Cameron, a known prostitute, was a violation of the law because he crossed state lines with her. Lucille was deeply in love with Johnson and knew he would marry her. Based on this she refused to cooperate with the authorities. The case fell apart.

Undaunted by their first failure, authorities arrested Johnson less than a month later. This time he was accused of transporting another known white prostitute, Belle Schreiber, across state lines, and this time it stuck. Belle was not in love with Johnson but certainly loved money, and he suspected authorities had paid her a pretty sum under the table to gain a conviction. Johnson's attorney argued vehemently, before a packed courtroom, that this particular course of prosecution was illegal on the face of it, since Johnson's involvement with Belle took place in 1909 and 1910 two years before the Mann Act was put in place. The attorney's argument, though valid, was ignored, and Johnson was convicted and sentenced to one year and one day in prison. Johnson was out on bail and had determined a course of action, the one he was executing this very day, to assure he did not do jail time.

Time in a federal prison was not appealing to Johnson, although, it was perhaps his time behind bars in Galveston, Texas that set the course for his mercurial rise to earn the distinction of being America's first Negro heavyweight boxing champion.

On February 25, 1901 Johnson participated in a fight against Joe Choynski who was well known in the area for his fighting skill. Johnson smiled as he remembered how inexperienced he was. Choynski had knocked him out in the third round. However, prize fighting was illegal in Texas during those years, and both he and Choynski were arrested and jailed. But perhaps due to Choynski's status in the community and Johnson's naiveté, Galveston police allowed the two men to go home at night as long as they promised to return to incarceration in the mornings. The sentence was twenty-five days for each man but the key to the whole deal was that the men had to spar everyday. Galveston residents would come each day to watch.

Over the course of those days, Choynski who was a Polish immigrant from California, had taken a real liking for Johnson and thought he saw some talent in the athletic young colored fighter. Johnson was willing to learn from him because Choynski had been singled out by Jim Jeffries as the only man who had seriously hurt him with a punch. This was extraordinary because Choynski weighed at best just over 175 pounds but would only fight in heavyweight bouts. Choynski used stealth and speed to confound his much heavier opponents, and Johnson adapted Choynski's fighting style, fashioning it to create his own unique style.

But in federal prison, he would not be afforded the same arrangements as Galveston police had given him, and he suspected he would face cruelty from prison guards. No, he must do this and do it now, so he got out of his car and strode into the tiny office where the dry-dock's day-to-day activities occurred. An older man with a tough looking leather-like face stood behind the desk.

"I'm Jack Johnson. I believe Diamond Jim Colosimo may have called ahead to make some arrangement," Johnson said to the man, while sliding two crisp $100 bills toward him.

"A Mr. Torrio did tell me that I should be expecting a gentleman named John Jackson to come by to make arrangements about having a roadster packed and shipped to Europe, first stop England I believe," the leather-faced man said. "You did say your name was John Jackson, right?"

Johnson remembered that in order to leave the country, he could not use his real name. He agreed to the arrangements orchestrated by Torrio and Colosimo that were devised to help Johnson leave the country. Torrio and Colosimo had experience in helping people "skip out on bail" because so often, one of their gangsters had to leave the country when it appeared they would be convicted of a capital crime after performing a sanctioned hit for "The Outfit."

"Correct," Johnson said never batting an eyelash. "The roadster is parked out front."

The Outfit controlled the Chicago dry-docks and no doubt the leather-faced man was either a part of the Mafia or an associate. He assured Johnson he would handle the arrangements "personally" and drove the roadster to the back of the office building. Johnson placed a kiss on his fingers and touched his beloved roadster. He hoped having it placed in a shipping crate and shipped to Europe would not produce any scratches. He longed to drive his roadster on the European open roads, free from adhering to speed limits.

"I'll see you in Europe, baby," Johnson said, as if bidding goodbye to a lover.

The silent colored man who had kidnapped Altamont's friend pulled up in his car, and Johnson got in. As they rode several blocks down, Johnson noticed two suspicious-looking white men walking down an alley to the back of a jewelry store. Johnson knew it was after business hours and such behavior seemed odd to Johnson. It was not his problem, he thought, and looked away, convincing himself this was a matter for the police.

Part Two

Kessler and Wilson froze for a second as the car passed leery that it might be the police.

"No, it's just two colored men passing in a car," Kessler assured Wilson, and they continued stealth-like down the alley to a window in the back of the jewelry store.

"I ought to smack you Wilson," Kessler said. "I told you the whores at the Double Deuce couldn't be trusted. But no, you couldn't just pay the money and go. No you had to take the diamond we risked our lives for and show it off. She gives you some free service, gets you drunk and steals the thing right from under your nose."

"I'm sorry," Wilson said half-heartedly.

Kessler still had the memory fresh in his mind. They never let the prostitute know they suspected she had stolen the gem. He had Wilson coax the prostitute to meet him at a bar for a night out on the town and they had paid Victoria Colosimo money so she could leave the Double Deuce and have drinks with Wilson. Wilson bought her back-to-back drinks for almost two hours and the prostitute got drunk quickly per their plan. Kessler sat patiently and watched then signaled for Wilson to convince the woman to leave the bar and return to the Double Deuce. Instead, he and Wilson pushed the woman into a waiting taxicab and drove her to a deserted warehouse. There Kessler took pleasure in the frightened moans of the woman as he tortured her to find out what she did with the diamond. She denied knowing anything about the diamond but as her pain increased she finally gave in and admitted to stealing it. His disgust grew deeper when she revealed she had taken it to a jeweler and gotten a miniscule payout for a gem worth a quarter million dollars. The jeweler had played her well, telling her the diamond was a fake, but he would give her money for her troubles. She was so dumb she fell for it. The woman spat blood from her bleeding mouth and told Kessler she watched the man place the diamond in a locked drawer in his desk in a back room.

Now here they hid just outside the jeweler store determined to break in and steal back the gem. Wilson begged him not to kill the prostitute so Kessler released her. Unfortunately, she went back to Diamond Jim Colosimo and Joe Torrio and said she was tortured and raped, conveniently leaving out her theft of the diamond. While the prostitute's description of Kessler was vague, The Outfit had put the word on the streets that a man matching Kessler's description, a man with a South African accent, was to be found and brought to Torrio for a nice financial reward. Wilson, in all his wisdom, had also told her he was of South African descent, so the woman had connected his accent to that of Wilson's.

But the rather large "blood diamond"* stolen from the diamond mines in South Africa was Kessler's ticket to a lifetime of wealth, and he was not going to allow Wilson's weakness for whores ruin his chance. In the back of his mind, he contemplated murdering Wilson some time after this was all over. He feared Wilson might do something less correctable. Kessler had no qualms about murder. He killed the man who had shared with him the secret that he was in possession of a mysterious diamond smuggled into America from South Africa. The man was not an educated man, and he had asked Kessler its value, since Kessler was from South Africa. Having already spilled one man's blood to obtain the precious gem, spilling Wilson's blood would be no problem, especially after this act of stupidity.

The plan was that Kessler would divert the attention of the clerk, who was working inside the jewelry store during the day, while Wilson stuck a small block of wood in an unseen area of the window. They had cased the jewelry store a day before and noticed that the clerk opened the window when he arrived to work because he suffered from allergies and closed it when he left. The small piece of wood prevented the window from closing completely, but without a careful examination, it appeared that the latch was locked. As expected in the clerk's haste, he heard the latch click, and assumed the window was secured but it was not. The window opened with no problem but Wilson was holding a bottle of liquor that dropped below the window as they climbed inside. Once inside, on the way toward the backroom door, the men passed large quantities of the jewelry encased in glass.

"Why don't we smash the glass casings and grab some other jewelry while we're here?" Wilson had suggested.

"One act of stupidity is enough on your part for the week, Wilson," Kessler said sarcastically. "If we steal any of those jewels we'll have not only the Mafia looking for us but the police as well. If we just steal our jewel back the owner won't dare to report it to the police, since even he should not have possession of it. How would he explain it?"

This was too easy Kessler said to himself as he took a large flathead screwdriver and forcibly pried the locked door open. Why hadn't the owner put the jewel in the safe? Perhaps he feared an employee might spot the blood diamond and alert the authorities? The answer to Kessler's question was apparent as an alarm inside the upscale jewelry store went off with a loud clatter.

"Damn, didn't you say there was no alarm Wilson?" asked Kessler, with great distress. "It was your responsibility to check for an alarm!"

"It must have been hidden. My surveillance of the place and the buildings plans didn't indicate there was one," Wilson replied.

The gorgeous jewel Kessler sought was there in the desk drawer. Kessler scooped up the purple velour pouch and securely placed it in his pants pocket.

"Let's get out of here," Kessler said.

The two thieves bolted for the window and climbed out. As they made their way to the street, a Chicago police officer called for them to halt and fired a warning shot. The duo tore down the street that led to the Chicago dry-docks with the police officer in hot pursuit.

Blocks away, a conversation between two colored dockworkers was concluding.

"Mr. Johnson sure got a raw deal with that Mann Act conviction. Them white folks always trying to keep colored folks down," said one of the dockworkers. "I don't blame him, I'd leave the country too."

Johnson, before leaving, had spotted the twosome and peeled out a wad of cash and handed each man a $100 bill.

"My brothers, if anyone should ask whose roadster car is

being shipped, you don't know a thing," Johnson told them.

"Our lips are sealed, Mr. Johnson," the colored men promised.

As Johnson disappeared down the street in the car that had pulled up and collected him, the two colored men, wild with joy because of their sudden financial windfall, decided to celebrate. One of the gentlemen pulled out a flask full of whiskey.

"This calls for a celebration," he said and the two dockworkers retreated to their favorite drinking hideaway.

As the two men disappeared, one block away the jewel thieves came up with a plan, still running for their lives, as the police officer shot bullets that whizzed past their heads.

"Let's split up," Kessler said. Kessler continued in the direction of the docks. Wilson peeled away and headed for an alley at an adjourning street. The police officer turned the corner, missed seeing Wilson, but was in time to get a bead on Kessler and fired another shot. As Kessler made it to the docks he turned right and spotted the roadster. He was out sight long enough to stash the jewels securely in the roadster's undercarriage and continued running. Within minutes the officer had him cornered on an open slip dock, and two more police officers appeared to assist him. Kessler surrendered.

Chicago detectives spent hours interrogating him but Kessler remembering that Wilson had dropped the liquor bottle below the window. Kessler told the police he and a friend were sharing a drink in the alley when the alarm went off, and that his friend had been so frightened he dropped the bottle. Kessler held to his story and insisted that he and his friend were not in the building and only ran because of the alarm. He lied, telling them he didn't know the other guy's name since they had just met and had combined money to buy a bottle of whiskey. The detectives released him, since they could not find the jewels on him and a team of beat officers failed to find the jewel on the docks after an exhaustive search. They did find the liquor bottle, which gave some credence to Kessler's story, but the police officers still had their doubts.

It was still dark when the cool Chicago wind brushed Kessler's face as he left the police station. Wilson reunited with Kessler at the hotel and they decided to wait until morning to go retrieve the jewel from the roadster. Kessler was glad it was he who had gotten cornered by the police instead of Wilson. Wilson would have folded under the intense interrogation. He would have told the police everything. Wilson was a liability, but Kessler determined he could not kill him yet; he might still need him.

The next morning when the duo arrived at the dry-docks, Wilson and Kessler received disturbing news.

"Why do you want to know about that roadster?" asked one of the colored dockworkers who had talked with Johnson the night before.

For Kessler this made him suspect the colored dockworker knew something. He pulled out a pistol, grabbed the colored man by the collar, and placed the pistol to his right temple.

"I'm not going to ask again you frigging *kaffer*.* Where is that roadster?" Kessler said.

"Gone."

Kessler pulled the trigger back.

"Where is it headed? Who owns it?" Kessler demanded.

Jack Johnson had given him $100 dollars to keep silent, but his life was at stake. Johnson would understand.

"It's headed to England. It belongs to the great Jack Johnson and I'm sure he's gone too."

Kessler pushed the colored dockworker to the ground. Kessler looked at Wilson with utter disdain.

"Damn. Looks like we're headed to England," Kessler said.

Chapter 4

Jack Johnson's wife Lucille had argued over making the trip to London and refused to go when she found out he had rented a flat on Sidney Street in the east End of London. She wasn't happy that the Mann Act conviction forced them to flee Chicago and move to Canada.

"I hear that no decent Brit will visit Sidney Street let alone live there," Lucille had told him. "That area, and most of the East End is full of low-lifes and criminals."

"We just moved to Canada from Chicago baby," Johnson quipped with a laugh. "Who do you think lived in Chicago?" He knew she wasn't going to accompany him on this trip to England, but he had to go. He needed to make some money.

But Johnson knew full well the real reason he wanted to live on Sidney Street while he conducted meetings with some British boxing officials who said they "wanted to explore the possibilities of staging Johnson in some exhibition fights."

He was a fugitive on the run from America where awaited him one year and one day in a federal penitentiary. His London flat had a full view of the street from both sides. If an American or British lawman were to walk that street they would stand out and Johnson would notice them. He hated living in fear, constantly looking over his shoulder, but that was the bed he had made for himself by outraging white America. They couldn't beat him in the ring so they made him a criminal.

Johnson left his flat to go to a nearby bar. He wanted to talk to the owner and see if he could get permission to cook food for himself. He missed American style food. He glanced around the bar and saw no man he feared. His brutish body and huge hands perhaps intimidated them. Certainly after spending time around Chicago's most dangerous mobsters and criminals he had learned correct body language to exhibit in a dangerous environment. The message was clear: Mess with me and get your head bashed in.

There were two people of interest for Johnson, or more like, the interest was more theirs towards him. A colored man stood near the pub window glancing in at him from time to time. The man even gave a nod hello but then turned his head quickly before Johnson could nod back. Inside the bar a somewhat attractive white woman with brown eyes and brunette hair kept batting her eyelashes at him. Johnson hadn't determined whether he would take her to bed yet, that depending on her conversation and if she was "for hire." He motioned with his head for her to join him and she did. He instructed the bartender to buy her another drink on him, and the bartender never asked the woman what she wanted. She was obviously a regular.

"I've never seen you here before," she said with a British accent.

"I'm not from here," Johnson answered.

"Aww, a colored American no less," she said coyly. "Most colored Brits don't have the money to buy anything in here. They usually stand outside begging for money from patrons who come or leave."

"I'm not most colored Americans or Brits," Johnson said, slapping on the bar a wad of British 50 pound notes. "Wouldn't you say?"

The woman's eyes widened and then narrowed. She was definitely interested in getting to know Johnson better. The look in her eyes also told Johnson she could be bought.

"That's a lot of money for a man alone to be walking with on Sidney Street," the woman said. "There are a lot of dangerous people out there."

"Not as dangerous as me," Johnson said, peeling back his suit jacket to reveal an American made pistol for the woman to see. There was also a protrusion in his trousers that the open jacket revealed.

"Both of those look dangerous to me," said the woman with a coy smile.

Johnson showed a huge grin as his gold tooth glistened from the sunlight with that statement and he pulled his jacket back in place. From the corner of his eye, he saw the colored man gazing in at him again. Johnson wondered if he and the white woman were in league together. Had she identified a "mark" and her partner, the leering colored man outside, would rob him as he left the bar? Or perhaps she had a different partner, someone inside the bar? Even though his libido was active, Johnson was having second thoughts about leaving to go anywhere with this woman. The last thing he needed would be to have to shoot someone in self defense. Americans were descendants of the Brits, and the apple doesn't fall far from the tree from his perspective. The Brits would be just as hateful to him in a court of law as the Americans. It was Johnson's intention to avoid finding out.

The woman turned out to be quite a talker, however. She told Johnson about "The Siege of Sidney Street" that occurred on January 2, 1911. Good Lord, the woman could talk! She told him about some anarchist who tried to lead a revolution that ended with the deaths of two members of a purportedly politically-motivated gang of burglars and international anarchists, supposedly led by Peter Piatkow, a.k.a. "Peter the Painter*." To Johnson it sounded like the people she talked about would have been comfortable on the southside of Chicago. He had grown tired of her babbling. The more she drank, the more she talked. He bought the woman another drink and thanked her for the company. He approached a waiter.

"Where is the owner," Johnson asked a waiter.

Upon finding the owner, Johnson paid him handsomely for the privilege of entering the kitchen and to fry some chicken, Southern style. The owner was impressed with the taste of the chicken and begged for the recipe. Johnson gave it to him after eliciting a promise that he be allowed to come to the pub and cook without cost whenever he pleased. The owner agreed. Johnson thanked him, wrapped his chicken securely in some butcher's paper, placed the package under his arm, and exited on to Sidney Street.

The colored man who had been leering at him now stood on the other side of the street. He didn't make eye contact with Johnson. Johnson stretched his arms over his head allowing his suit jacket to open wide so the fellow could see the gun. Poverty was evident throughout the street as he walked. The woman was right about the area. Some of the men on the street looked to be some of the most unsavory characters one could see in any place in the world, and according to her, the streets on London's East End were full of these types.

As Johnson walked briskly towards his flat, he noticed the colored man from outside the pub crossing the street to intersect him. As Johnson stopped with intentions to confront the colored man and ask why he was following him, the first round from a hunting rifle filled the air, missing Johnson's head by inches. Johnson began to run in a hunched position making his way to his flat. A second round from the rifle kicked up a storm of dust directly in front of him. The colored man ran to him and clutched his arm.

"Follow me," the man told Johnson in a distinct British accent. Johnson soon learned that no one knew the back alleys of London's East End better than this man who had countless times lost pursuers from Scotland Yard after a botched heist. The colored Brit led Johnson through the many mazes of the alleyways, and as they turned a corner, a man stepped into their paths. Johnson recognized him immediately, but the colored Brit looked confused.

"Altamont! Boy I'm glad to see you!" Johnson said, clutching Altamont's hand.

The colored Brit didn't recognize the man until he spoke to Johnson.

"Sorry to welcome you to England under such a stressful situation, Mr. Johnson" Altamont said to Johnson.

"So nice to see you again Mr. Steve Dixie*," Altamont said, but the voice was unmistakable. At that point Dixie recognized the voice of Mr. Sherlock Holmes.

"Is that you, Mr. Holmes?" Dixie asked.

Johnson saw Altamont ignore Dixie's question. Johnson wondered why Dixie had called Altamont, "Mr. Holmes? "We must move quickly," Altamont said. "I'm afraid we've uncovered a terrible business here, my friends."

Dixie looked dumbfounded, while at the same time, Johnson's mind was reeling. Johnson wondered, was this indeed the great Sherlock Holmes?

"Your name is Steve Dixie?" Johnson inquired of the colored Brit. "Why were you watching me, following me?"

"I recognized you. I am a boxer myself. I couldn't resist the chance you might teach me a few tricks of the trade Mr. Johnson," Dixie said. "I had just worked up enough nerve to approach you and introduce myself. I wanted to see if you could give me some pointers. Then someone started shooting at you."

"You know this man Altamont, or should I say Mr. Holmes?"

"I do and Mr. Johnson, I am in as delicate situation now, with those Irish thugs, as I was in Chicago. I need you to continue addressing me as Altamont for the time being," Altamont answered. "However, until today, I thought Steve Dixie's thievery and grifting had sent him on an irreversible path of destruction. That was until I saw him risk his life to remove you from harm's way. I can now only conclude there are some redeemable characteristics still there. But enough small talk for the moment, follow me."

Altamont didn't see Dixie smiling, but Johnson did, as Dixie ran up the rear of the duo protecting the backs of the two men through the maze. Something told Johnson Dixie's life would never be the same after this night. Within minutes they were perched securely in the flophouse apartment Altamont was working out of.

"I've been following you for most of the day," Altamont said to Johnson. "I heard you were in London and set my task to finding you immediately. I went to your East End apartment and found your door slightly ajar. As I entered, it was clear by the way your abode was ransacked, that someone was in a frantic search for something they hoped would be there."

Johnson's face showed confusion and concern.

"Don't worry," Altamont said, laying a hand on the boxer's broad shoulder. "I will find out who your nemesis is, but I'm afraid that before I'm done, I'll find there is more than one villain in this plot."

"I bet it's your Irish friend in America, the one that I kidnapped before the exhibition fight against the redhead last year," Johnson said, obviously doing his best impression of deduction per Sherlock Holmes style. "Is he in England?

"He was irate upon his release but it is not him," Altamont said. "I know firsthand he is in Ireland. No, it is someone else for sure and we must wrap this mystery up as swiftly as possible. I myself am headed to Ireland in two days."

Altamont stood and walked to the door before turning and sniffing the air.

"Is that some of the fried chicken I sampled during my visit at the Café de Champion in Chicago? Might I have a piece to take with me?" Altamont asked.

Johnson let out a hearty laugh, as he unwrapped his package of food to reveal several pieces of Southern fried chicken. Altamont snagged a piece of the breast and returned quickly to the door. "It is best neither of you leave the room until I return," Altamont said

When the door closed on Altamont's departure, Johnson turned to Dixie and offered the colored Brit a piece of chicken as well. Dixie grabbed a leg and smiled as he chewed.

"Now that's good yard bird," Dixie said. "So you met Mr. Holmes in Chicago?"

"Yes, I met him as Altamont in Chicago when he came to eat at my restaurant. We shared dinner and an opera one night and a fight and dinner the next night. For the life of me I'm having a hard time accepting the fact I was in the presence of the great detective Sherlock Holmes," Johnson said, shaking his head. "That explains why he knew so much about me. He even said I would perhaps meet Sherlock if I ever made it to London. No doubt with his unlimited resources, Altamont, or should I say Sherlock Holmes, was able to keep tabs on me. He knew I was in England."

Johnson's expression changed from pleasure to concern as he continued. "I believe the gentleman who just left is up to his neck in some really dangerous things. I could endanger him even more if I continue further conversations without referring to him as Altamont."

"If you met him as Altamont then Mr. Holmes is undercover, doing God knows what," Dixie said. "You are right to continue calling him Altamont. As far as his being in danger, that's what makes Mr. Holmes who he is. That's what gives the man life, living his life under danger and stress, always staying steps ahead of his opponent. He wouldn't have it any other way and trust me, like a cat with nine lives, Mr. Holmes has escaped sure death at the hands of some of Europe's greatest criminals by pure cunning."

From that point on, Dixie shared Johnson's chicken and marveled at the food so famous and acclaimed among people in the southern region of North America.

As they finished their one-course meal, Johnson gazed upon Dixie curiously. "I don't want to pry Mr. Dixie, but I believe Altamont doesn't trust you."

"You're right, and I don't blame him for it" Dixie replied. "I met Mr. Holmes over a decade ago. I ran with a group of criminals called the Spencer John gang that was led by a ruffian named Barney Stockdale. I was hired to intimidate Mr. Holmes, scare him off of a case he was considering to investigate."

Johnson let out a loud laugh. "For some reason, I don't think you were successful. Altamont has dealt with so many criminal types, I'm sure he's unflappable."

"You're so right," Dixie agreed. "In fact, he turned the whole situation on me and frightened me. He told me if I didn't back off, he might reopen the investigation into the Perkins murder affair that happened at the Holborn Bar. I couldn't chance him doing so. When Sherlock Holmes starts investigating a fellow, bad things happen."

Johnson nodded his head, understanding it would be uncomfortable to continue along the path of their conversation. Dixie obviously had a dark secret in his past that he just assume leave there. Johnson had taken a liking to Dixie though; there seemed to be some real good in him. Dixie had just taken up with the wrong folks. Johnson also realized Dixie wanted to change the topic, diverting the conversation to something of great interest to both of them.

"I believe for Altamont's safety, Mr. Dixie, you should get used to calling him Altamont," Johnson said. Dixie nodded his head in agreement, then spoke.

"Now that I have you all to myself, as I told you, I'm a boxer as well, and would love for you to show me some tricks of the trade? Help me improve?" Dixie asked sheepishly. "And tell me a little about yourself, about your boxing career? How did you start fighting?"

Johnson emitted a hearty laugh. "My career started in 1897 when I beat up a local bully in my hometown of Galveston, Texas. I fought some local fights and then I ended up in a Texas jail with Joe Choyinski. Choyinski taught me some things that have made me the champion I am now. Here, let me show you what I mean." Johnson motioned for Dixie to stand up. "Assume your defensive stance."

For one-half hour, Johnson taught Dixie how to attack, demonstrated different defensive stances, and gave him a few new wrinkles on how to be a better offensive fighter. They stopped to sit and rest, sweat pouring from their brown faces. Johnson smiled as he spoke, a sort of sadness in his voice. "My boxing skills are God given I admit, though my conduct is not godly," Johnson said. "Mr. Dixie, you like I, have a brown face. My knowledge of colored folks here in England is limited, but I'm not sure if your heritage includes one of slavery. Colored Americans have evolved from a legacy of slavery and bigotry and though we are now a free people, we are still not considered equal to white men in America."

"Don't fool yourself, Mr. Johnson. The white folks who started in America were descendants of folks here in England. There's a large majority of England's population who share the same feeling of superiority over the colored population here on our fair shores," Dixie said. "Slavery existed here as well."

Johnson conceded to the point Dixie made with a knowing nod of his head. "When I met Altamont in Chicago last year, he called me an "anomalous" character. He meant in essence, a colored man doing what I do, and being who I am, should simply not exist in this era. I don't just beat white men up in the ring, I taunt them, loom over them as they lay prostate from one of my lethal punches. When that happens, white men in America become afraid. They fear they will be revealed as weaker than colored men in the public eye."

Dixie nodded as Johnson continued. "I beat Tommy Burns on Christmas Day in 1908, to win the heavyweight boxing championship, and I beat him bad, Mr. Dixie. He was bloodied while laying there in the ring, and I talked down to him, taunted him. It took a lot of persuasion from white promoters to get Burns in the ring with me. He knew he couldn't beat me and he didn't want to be in there with me. I saw the fear in his eyes. It took them a few years to actually concede the championship to me after that. As a result of winning the championship, I became rich, and flaunted my relationships with white women publicly. The white power structure saw me as downright disobedient. In reality, Mr. Dixie, I am white America's worst nightmare."

Johnson's whole body slumped at that point, perhaps from a long day, perhaps from the shock of being shot at, perhaps from the conversation, most likely from all three. "I'm really tired Mr. Dixie," Johnson said. "Can we resume this conversation at a later date?"

Dixie conceded the bed to the American champion and

he fixed himself a pallet on the floor. Soon they fell asleep.

Chapter 5

Johnson awoke with sunshine from a tiny slit in the window burning furiously in his face. He raised his arm to shield his eyes from the bright rays. He soon arose and walked to Dixie, awakening him.

"Did Altamont say what time he would be returning?" Johnson asked.

Dixie raised his head slightly and hunched his shoulders to show he had no answer. The clock read 9:15 a.m. Altamont walked in.

"Altamont, glad you got here. I have to get back to my apartment," Johnson said while stretching his arms as he stood.

"I have Scotland Yard inspectors doing a discreet search of your apartment," Altamont told Johnson. "I suspect that other than someone wanting you dead, you have something in your possession that perhaps another party wants badly. Bad enough, in fact, they ransacked your apartment in search of it, Mr. Johnson. Did you bring something from America that belongs to someone else?"

"I assure you, Altamont, I have no idea why someone would ransack my apartment. I only bought my best suits and clothing and I had one of my roadsters shipped here as well."

"Then the solution to your mysterious physical and personal attacks lies somewhere with those items, I assure you," Altamont said. "But if you possess something someone wants, why would they try and shoot you? It only stands to reason there are two different motives at play in this scenario."

Altamont turned to Dixie. "We are going to have to put Mr. Johnson under a twenty-four-hour watch, Mr. Dixie. Have you any resources to make such a thing happen?"

Dixie's mind started churning with various options. Years of being a rogue and grifter had placed him in the company of England's East Side's seediest characters. Then it dawned on him. "You know Altamont, I have a cousin in the lower East End of London. Among the colored underworld, with whom I associate, he is known as 'The Fixer.' He has made many dead bodies happen and some simply disappear over the years. Don't put me on a court stand to testify to that, please. And he has been known to hire out. He and his band of thugs will provide protection for whatever entity needs it at times. I could probably get him and his thugs to watch over Mr. Johnson for a nominal fee."

"Excellent, Mr. Dixie. The Fixer, as you call him and his men must be like shadows, however, and work undetected for the meantime. If they do run across any potential suspects, I simply want them followed and not confronted," Altamont said. "Also, I'll need you to wire a telegraph to my dear American friend, Mr. Harry Houdini, in New York. I think we will have to flush Mr. Johnson's stalkers out into the open. I have just the plan. You, Mr. Johnson, once we place you under surveillance, must hide for a day or so. In fact, I know exactly the place you can stay. A very attractive lady who I've crossed paths with in the past will see that you are comfortable."

Johnson noticed that Mr. Holmes was pleased Dixie had referred to him as Altamont. It showed that Dixie now understood the perilous game in front of them and felt an urgency to protect Holmes' identity, as did Johnson. Johnson believed that Dixie wanted to do everything right in this situation to show Altamont that he did have positive redeeming characteristics.

Johnson interrupted the conversation. "Gentlemen, I'm honored that you are taking such measures to protect me in this matter, and while I'm sure your colored East End associates are highly capable of protecting me, at least for a temporary period, I would much rather have Americans cover my back, people I can recognize myself, so that I don't confuse my protectors with my enemies. I have a friend in Chicago who owes me a favor so I will send a telegram to him as well. You met him Altamont, Diamond Jim Colosimo. He'll send someone to protect me. I'm sure of that much," Johnson said.

Johnson pulled out his billfold, thumbed through and extracted a business card. He scribbled his message hurriedly and handed it to Dixie. Dixie sneaked a peek at the name of the person to whom it was addressed: Diamond Jim Colosimo. Dixie knew nothing of him.

"Here, Mr. Johnson, have your American cohorts come to this address when he arrives in London," Altamont said, handing Johnson a paper with an address written upon it.

Altamont wrote his telegram and then handed it to Dixie. The addressee on Altamont's was familiar to Dixie however: Harry Houdini the world famed magician.

Altamont brought food for the men when he arrived. After receiving his instructions, Dixie ate quickly so he could execute his task. The great Sherlock Holmes had just entrusted him with a critical assignment and he did not plan to fail.

"Mr. Johnson, I've brought you food from 'our neck of the woods' as you Southerners in the United States would say,"

Altamont said with a weary smile. It was obvious he was tired from the case he was working on and now the added responsibility of taking on the burden of helping Johnson.

Johnson was curious just what Altamont was working on, in relation to the Irishmen, but didn't ask. Whatever it was, it was an elaborate mission that required Altamont to travel to America, back to England and now in two days, to Ireland. Johnson could also tell time was catching up to Altamont. He was much older and his hyper energetic zeal was not as prevalent as in the days of the adventures chronicled by Dr. Watson.

"Altamont, doesn't bother you that you are now in alliance with two colored men?" Johnson asked. "With me being a fugitive and Mr. Dixie a thief, decent white men would probably find such a notion irreprehensible."

Altamont smiled and retrieved a small safety pen from his desk. He pricked his right index finger with it, causing blood to appear.

"You do the same, Mr. Dixie and Mr. Johnson," Altamont said, handing over the safety pen.

Johnson and Dixie pricked their fingers and red droplets of blood oozed out.

"Is not your blood the color of mine?" Altamont asked.

Johnson and Dixie nodded.

"Then the conclusion is elementary, Mr. Johnson," Altamont said. "Though our skin colors differ, we are all three human beings with red blood coursing through our veins. In essence, God created us all the same."

Johnson's jaw dropped. This was unbelievable. A white

man admitting that a colored man was an equal. But this was no ordinary man, Johnson thought with a smile. This was the great Sherlock Holmes.

Then Mr. Johnson extended his bloody index finger towards Altamont. "Then let our blood intermingle as brothers." Johnson was testing Altamont for true conviction of what he said.

Altamont and Dixie, without hesitation, extended their bloody fingertip and intermingled their fingers with Johnson's.

"Equals we are," Altamont said. "Now that we have pledged an alliance as brothers, Mr. Dixie I have only two days left before heading to Ireland. We have limited time to solve this mystery. Allow me to send this one last instruction with you."

Altamont took a seat at his desk and began writing. Within minutes he stood and walked towards Dixie, handing him the rest of his instructions.

Part Two

The morning's weather was gray and overcast and small pellets of rain fell on Dixie's face. He didn't fear being recognized by Johnson's potential assassins because it had been within split-second timing that Dixie had intervened and pulled Johnson through the alleyway. Dixie's back had been to the assailant, and it was dark. Nevertheless, for safety sake, he followed back streets and alleys to get to the telegraph office.

After reading the messages Altamont and Johnson sent to Chicago and New York, the agent peered over his glasses curiously at Dixie. "I thought Mr. Holmes was out of town?" he growled.

"He is," Dixie said. "Mr. Watson, however, has forbidden me to say anything more about that subject. Please be sure to send the telegraphs immediately."

Dixie wheeled around and left quickly to avoid more questions, hoping the agent believed they were being sent at the behest of Dr. Watson for Holmes.

It took Dixie ten minutes to get to his next destination near a row of abandoned warehouses. A colored sentry searched him when he arrived at the last building. Dixie thought to himself that The Fixer and his criminal enterprise must have moved up significantly in finances and status since they last saw each other. Dixie was then escorted to an office in the back of the warehouse. Upon seeing Dixie; his cousin stood from behind his desk, walked around and embraced him.

The Fixer stood just over six feet tall, had a wiry build, dark mysterious eyes, and very full lips. His complexion was dark chocolate and the side of his clean-shaven face bore a healed knife scar. "Cousin Dixie, you old rogue, what brings you here to see your lowly little cousin?" The Fixer asked.

Dixie glared back at the young thug who sat across from The Fixer. The thug glared back at Dixie, trying to intimidate him. Dixie had seen the type before. They look and talk tough, but punched like a woman. In less than three seconds the thug simply rolled my eyes away from Dixie without speaking. Dixie was the senior criminal in the room and the young thug knew his place in the criminal hierarchy.

"I'm here on business, cousin," Dixie said. "There is a very important colored man here from America that needs protection."

Dixie dropped a wad of bills on the desk. The cousin counted them then he looked up. "I'm definitely interested in hearing more. His name wouldn't happen to be Mr. Jack Johnson, would it?"

Dixie nodded my head. He glanced over at the young thug, not sure he wanted to talk in front of him. The thug seemed to get the message, as he got up and left without comment. The cousin continued speaking. "Some white American man came here two nights ago. They wanted to hire me to locate and follow Mr. Johnson and asked, if need be, would I be willing to kill him. I refused him. I don't spy on colored folks or kill them for that matter for the sake of some white man. I've read about what they're doing to him in America. Those white boys are something in that country. I'll take the job. Mr. Johnson will be safe enough under my protection."

"Did the white man give you his name?" Dixie asked.

Though Dixie was no Sherlock, it would be a safe bet this was the person who fired rifle shots at Johnson the evening prior.

"This one was real slick, didn't say much and definitely didn't identify himself. He wore a Cowboy hat though," The Fixer said.

"Well, give as best description you can of him to your people so they can be on the look out for him. Let's hope he's stupid enough to continue wearing the cowboy hat," Dixie said.

"I can describe his partners too," The Fixer said.

"There were other men with him?" Dixie asked with surprise.

"Yeah, two men were with him. Both Brits, one colored and the other white," The Fixer said. "I've seen them both in the streets before, both real low level thugs. I think they are the ones who brought the American to me. Nothing happens on the East End that I or my boys don't see, I think they knew that," The Fixer said, with a sense of pride in his voice.

"Well I'm glad you're siding with your gray-haired cousin," Dixie said. "It has been a while since we teamed up. Believe me, cousin; we are on the correct side of things of this situation."

Dixie gave his cousin as much information as he thought he would need to do the job, and then hurried away. He knew Holmes would want to know what he discovered. Dixie thought it curious that the young thug, in his cousin's office, excused himself just after he told The Fixer he was in league with Jack Johnson. Was it because the young thug sensed Dixie wanted privacy? He didn't think the guy was that perceptive. He didn't like or trust the arrogant punk.

However, Dixie's mistrust proved right. The young punk had left Dixie and his cousin to bargain away a debt owed in the streets. "The Rat" went to a pub several blocks down and told a street thug called The Weasel about Dixie's visit. Since he knew where Dixie lived, he also gave him Dixie's address. The Rat had heard The Weasel say aloud in the pub he would forgive anyone's debt or owe a favor if they could produce any information about Jack Johnson's whereabouts. The Weasel was thankful for the financially valuable information and assured the colored street punk his debt, from a previous transaction, was erased for providing such valuable information. The Weasel left the pub directly behind The Rat. It was time to get paid!

The man named Kessler paced up and down the floor of the East End hotel room's confined space. His friend Wilson sat on one of the twin beds and watched the huge Kessler acutely, seeing the rage building within the volatile man. His round white face was reddening, and then he suddenly exploded. "How in the world does a colored man the size of Jack Johnson just disappear in thin air right in the middle of East End, London?" Kessler bellowed.

"He obviously had help," Wilson replied. "You saw him duck into the alleyway with the other colored fellow right?"

Wilson and Kessler had taken turns watching and following Johnson, and his stepping out to the bar allowed a thorough search of his room. They didn't find what they were looking for. They left the room hastily when the gunfire on Sidney Street erupted.

"We need to find out who that colored fellow was. I'm sure he's a Brit," Kessler said. "He's toast if I get my hands on him, just like Johnson will be."

"The jewel we're looking for has still got to be in the undercarriage of his car. All we need are the keys," Wilson said.

"Let's also assume Johnson has no idea they are there," Kessler returned. "Well, at least for his own sake, he had better have no idea they're there. We just need to get to the keys, break into the packing crate and everything will be fine. But we will kill him if need be." Kessler threw his loaded pistol on the bed.

"Well, I checked the dock before I came back here, and the metal crate with his roadster still hasn't been opened. The lock is still there," Wilson said. "You may be right that Johnson hasn't found them yet, but you never know. My fear is that the British custom inspectors may have found it."

Then there was a mild repetition of knocks on the door. Kessler pulled his pistol from the bed and moved behind the door as Wilson opened it.

A smallish man with a pimpled face spoke quietly. They recognized the voice as that of The Weasel, a local snitch they had approached to inquire about Johnson. "We spoke at the pub last night. You told me to contact you if there was any word of the colored American boxer. There is a buzz amidst the colored Brits down on the East End. There's talk some colored Brit named The Fixer and his henchmen have been hired to protect him."

"The Fixer? Protecting Johnson? Who in the hell is The Fixer?" blurted Wilson. Wilson quickly silenced himself when Kessler put his finger to his lips.

"And what of the colored fellow who is in league with Johnson. Who is he?" Kessler asked.

"A rogue and grifter named Steve Dixie seems to be the one who hired The Fixer," the pimpled-faced Brit answered. "I was under the impression you were paying for this information?"

Wilson reached in his pocket and handed the Brit an American fifty-dollar bill. The Weasel lifted it to the light examining for authenticity, since he dabbled in counterfeiting bills. Satisfied it was real, he continued sharing information. "Here's Dixie's last known address," said The Weasel as he handed Wilson a slip of paper and then left closing the door behind him. The two men grabbed their coats and caught a hansom to the address on the paper.

Dixie was less than a block from his flat and thought about Johnson and Altamont and how much he needed to reunite with them. He hadn't bothered to tell Johnson or Altamont where he was going after completing his errands since his intent was to slip into his flat, get the stash of money he had hidden, and return as quickly as possible. The money was substantial, his life savings, and he was going to use it to help Johnson pay The Fixer additional funds for protection. Once in the room, Dixie moved the desk to get under the floorboards. He had not yet exposed his hiding place when a large boot busted the door open.

"Steve Dixie, I presume," said Kessler as he entered Dixie's flat.

It was at this point Dixie realized the decision to try and run past Kessler, in an attempt to escape, was futile since Kessler held a pistol and so did Wilson who walked in behind him. Kessler was a huge man and Wilson stood even larger in stature than his partner. Without further words, Kessler lifted Dixie in the air and hurled him against the wall. It hurt. Dixie knew these men weren't leaving before doing more harm, and he knew all this had something to do with Jack Johnson.

"My good man, I have no idea who you are or how I've offended you but if it is an apology you want then I apologize," Dixie said as he looked squarely into Kessler's eyes. "I would rather not fight, but if it's a fight you're looking for, I'm afraid you've bitten off more than you can chew."

Kessler placed his gun in his waistband and took a few steps towards Dixie again, feigning a punch with his left fist to Dixie's head, which Dixie blocked, but Kessler countered with a right cross blow to Dixie's solar plexus, forcing all the wind out of Dixie, causing him to crumple on the floor. Wilson jumped in the fray, placing a booted foot against Dixie's temple. Dixie toppled to the floor.

Wilson walked up to the hapless Dixie, this time, placed his right index finger under Dixie's chin and lifting Dixie's face up so that we were eye to eye. "My friend Kessler here is not much of a talker as you can see and nor am I in the mood to chit chat. We want information that if you don't give to us, Kessler here may get overzealous. At times he tends to jump the gun and show people what will happen to them if they don't share information, just like now. In this case he didn't even ask. Get the message?" The stench of chewing tobacco coming from Wilson's mouth was foul and he bore a brownish yellow stain on his teeth.

"What is it that you want to know?" Dixie asked as his mind tried to clear cobwebs from his thoughts caused by

Wilson's kick while trying desperately to stand up and breathe after Kessler's punch. Dixie had been in this position before, a situation that had proven just as painful.

"Where is Jack Johnson, Dixie?" Kessler asked authoritatively.

"Who?" Dixie asked. Wilson enormous fist punched Dixie in the temple, knocking him back to the floor.

"I don't know any Jack Johnson except the champion boxer. Isn't he an American? Shouldn't you be looking in America?" Dixie said, trying to divert answering the question. No sooner had he finished speaking did he feel the full thrust of Kessler's knee connect beneath his chin, this time placing him flat on his back.

"This is going get a lot worst before it gets better," Wilson said. "We don't like *kaffers* anyway."

"Not sure what that means," Dixie said defiantly. "I bet they don't think much of you either." He braced himself for another act of violence.

Before Dixie could speak or the South Africans react, a familiar voice chimed from the doorway. "Let's go, Mr. Dixie, at this very instance," Dr. Watson said. The doctor stood in the entrance of the door with a revolver positioned to swivel and fire in either direction of the men.

"You my good man, Mr. Dixie, pick up that twine of rope beside the bed and lash these two gentlemen up," Dr. Watson said as he motioned the two men towards the chairs by the table in the room.

Dixie's head and stomach were still throbbing from the blows delivered by Kessler and Wilson but did as he was instructed. Dixie turned the two chairs so they were back-to-back and shoved Wilson and Kessler into each. He began tying the rope snugly around the men and then suddenly pulled the rope hard enough around the men to make Kessler winch with pain.

"My friend, why would you endanger your own life for this *kaffer*?" Wilson asked Dr. Watson. "Because when we get free we'll surely find you and him and inflict much pain on you both, if not kill you."

Dixie had heard enough. His fist came crashing down on Wilson's temple.

"Aw, you're South African?" Dr. Watson asked. "Mr. Dixie, I don't know if you were aware, but the word *kaffer* in South Africa is very derogatory to people of your color."

Upon hearing this, Dixie punched Kessler in the jaw this time. "Is that a fact? I think I just told Mr. Kessler what I think of that."

"I am from South Africa too," Wilson answered Dr. Watson. "And I'm a man of influence, whether there or in England."

"I doubt that," Dr. Watson said. "I, on the other hand, have friends in Scotland Yard, and I don't think you want me showing you what real influence feels like, because my dear sir, I would exert the full force of that influence squarely on you and your friend."

Watson eyed them carefully as Dixie finished securing his ropes around the two South Africans. "We must leave now, Mr. Dixie. Our mutual friend is awaiting our arrival." Dr. Watson walked to the door. Dixie followed him.

"Would that mutual friend be Jack Johnson?" Kessler asked.

Neither Dr. Watson nor Dixie answered, but Dixie turned from the door, made his my way to the loose floorboards beneath his desk, lifted a few floorboards, and scooped up the neatly bundled wads of cash he had stored in a brown paper bag. He had to run to catch Dr. Watson.

Kessler listened as Dr. Watson and Dixie plodded down the hallway.

"We'll cross paths again, you stupid *kaffer* and you meddling old fool," Kessler hollered.

Chapter 6

Dr. Watson was on the street waving for a hansom he had waiting. By that time, Dixie caught up to him. The two climbed into the seats, simultaneously emitting sighs of relief.

"No wonder Mr. Holmes has you as his sidekick," Dixie said. "Wow, you seem to show up at the right time in all of his other adventures. How did you know where I was and know I was in danger?"

Dr. Watson stared out the window while answering, somewhat nonchalantly. "Mr. Holmes asked me to find you since he thought it best to move Mr. Johnson to a location in West London. I saw you leave a warehouse, so I decided to follow you rather than approach you at the time. While Holmes may have found this sudden rush of trust in you, I know what a scoundrel you truly are. I thought you might try to double cross Holmes so I followed."

Reality struck Dixie at that moment. Not only must he prove to Holmes that he could be trusted to perform any task assigned, but he now had a more stubborn Dr. Watson whose trust he had to earn too. By Dr. Watson's tone of voice, it was going to be tough to do.

"When I saw you go into the flat, I watched to see to whom you would betray Holmes," Dr. Watson said. "I saw the two men approach your flat and thought I was correct in my assumption, but I knew you were in peril when the men kicked your door in. If those men had been allies they would have simply knocked. I would have come right away, but I had to instruct the hansom driver to wait and be prepared to make a hasty getaway. I was right, at least about the fact you were in peril. We have yet to see if you can really be trusted."

"Where in West London are we headed?" Dixie asked.

"To a nice woman's estate. Her name is Lucy Hebron,*" the doctor said.

The hansom ride from London's East End to the West End was one of silence between Dr. Watson and Dixie. To Dixie it seemed as if Dr. Watson resented being in his presence. Because of Dr. Watson's silence, Dixie believed Dr. Watson probably wouldn't be with him at all, let alone have saved him, had not Sherlock Holmes made the request. Dixie broke the silence as they neared a suburb just outside of West London. "Does *kaffer* really mean something derogatory in South Africa?"

Dr. Watson shifted uncomfortably, and continued to stare out the window as he spoke. "*Kaffer* is the South African equivalent of the American word *nigger*. I think it is ignorant to make up such names for anyone, but it is the way of our society."

The twosome finally arrived at Lucy Hebron's home and they exited after Dr. Watson paid the driver. He declined Dixie's offer to pay.

"Based on that confirmation, Dr. Watson, I sure hope the man, Kessler, and I do cross paths. I'll show him what a British *kaffer* will do when he doesn't have a gun pointed at him."

The woman who opened the door was as beautiful a woman Dixie had ever laid eyes on. "Dr. Watson, welcome. And can I assume you are Mr. Dixie?" Hebron asked shaking both Dr. Watson's and Dixie's hands. "Everyone was awaiting

77

your arrival. My name is Lucy Hebron. Welcome to my home. Follow me."

The men followed the shapely lady into a living room where Altamont and Mr. Johnson were seated. "Put your eyes back in your head," Dr. Watson told Dixie. "You look like a love struck teenager."

Dixie smiled. Dr. Watson's evaluation wasn't far off the mark. When Dr. Watson and Dixie entered the living room, in the background played a different type of music. Dixie had never heard it but the melodic sounds seemed to have Altamont and Johnson mesmerized. Johnson's face seemed to light up when Lucy Hebron entered. "What kind of music is that?" Dixie asked.

"I just returned from a visit to what Americans call the West Coast. I was visiting the state of California, and I was introduced to this form of music. Isn't it wonderful?" Hebron cooed.

"What is it called, if I might ask?" Dixie asked.

"Jazz*," Hebron replied.

"I've heard this type of music a few years ago but I don't really think it had a name then," Johnson said. "Earl Hines* was playing it at a club I attended in Pittsburgh, Pennsylvania just before the turn of the century."

The first impression of most observers would be that Lucy was a white woman. Johnson and Dixie however noticed the ever so subtle features of a black woman -- the full cheekbones, the sensual yet slightly full lips, and a posterior that protruded outwardly in a most titillating fashion.

"I've prepared sandwiches, gentlemen. I'll go to the

78

kitchen now and bring them out, now that Dr. Watson and Mr. Dixie are here," Hebron said. Johnson and Dixie couldn't help but watch the exquisitely beautiful woman glide gracefully out with the most thought provoking stride. Both men caught each other admiring the lovely Lucy Hebron, and then Johnson spoke.

"Take a number Mr. Dixie," Johnson said with a wide grin, as the woman disappeared. "I'm way ahead of you my friend." Both men snickered sheepishly, obviously both smitten with the beautiful Lucy Hebron. Watson observed the pathetic behavior of the colored men and shook his head. They both simply smiled at the good doctor.

Altamont cleared his throat loudly; snapping everyone's attention back to the room and him, but Dr. Watson spoke before anyone else could say anything. "I followed Mr. Dixie just to make sure he wasn't betraying us, and he didn't, at least not that time. I found Mr. Dixie at his flat, and found him just in the nick of time. Two South African goons had him cornered, and had I not interceded, Mr. Dixie was headed for quite a very serious beating."

"Mr. Dixie, say it ain't so! We practiced just the other night," Johnson said with a disappointed tone.

"There were two of them, Mr. Johnson, what could I do?" Dixie asked defensively. "They got the drop on me."

Despite Dixie's defense, Johnson shook his head.

"South African, you say?" Altamont asked, as he stood and began his infamous pace near the fireplace.

Then Dixie chimed in. "Yeah but in the conversation I had with The Fixer, he told me an American was accompanied by two Brits, one colored and one white. They came to him and wanted help finding and watching Mr. Johnson," Dixie said. "The American even pitched the idea he might want them to kill Mr. Johnson."

"What?" Johnson retorted. "This is getting too far out of hand. It was probably that cowboy who was shooting at me. I just hope he isn't a Texas boy. That would be the ultimate insult."

"This brings me back to my deduction that there are two entities involved in this game. I said that last night," Altamont said. "Even more obvious is they both have separate agendas. I believe more than ever the sooner my friend Harry Houdini responds to my telegram, the sooner we can get to the bottom of this treachery."

"It is strange though. The Fixer said one of the men wore a cowboy hat, and neither Kessler nor Wilson wore anything close to that. And there were no Brits with Kessler and Wilson when they roughed me up."

"You said Mr. Dixie was in trouble when you arrived?" Johnson asked Dr. Watson.

"Oh, yes, it seemed the ruffian Kessler had landed a punch into Mr. Dixie's solar plexus and doubled him over into a most helpless of positions," Dr. Watson answered, seeming to get a small pleasure out of announcing Dixie's dire dilemma.

"Oh my God, Mr. Dixie, I thought you said you were a boxer," Johnson said. "Any amateur knows to protect his solar plexus. When we sparred last night you seemed far more advanced than what I'm hearing."

"Remember when we were sparring last night, you kept feigning a punch to my head and countered with a jab to the stomach? You called it a weak point for me," Dixie reminded him.

"Awww, Mr. Dixie," Johnson said with disappointment, holding his head with both hands, "I thought we had corrected that."

"Did The Fixer mention anything about a South African accent?" Altamont asked.

"No," Dixie replied, faced still pained from letting Johnson down.

"We have more than one set of antagonists, Mr. Johnson. This is clear." Altamont turned his attention to Lady Hebron who was entering with the sandwiches. "I must leave, perhaps until morning Lady Hebron. I need to set my snares to capture our mysterious villains. Dr. Watson will accompany me as I try to resurrect some of my B Street Irregulars*. Lady Hebron, please see that Mr. Johnson and Mr. Dixie receive adequate lodging here for the night while we're gone. I will compensate you handsomely upon my return."

With that Altamont and Dr. Watson left to hail a hansom in search of the B Street Irregulars.

Chapter 7

As Holmes and Watson pulled off in their hansom, another hansom arrived. Four colored men exited and one ran to the door, knocking rapidly. Lady Hebron looked out, didn't recognize the men and called for Johnson and Dixie. Dixie peered through the curtain and recognized the young colored Brit as the warehouse sentry who frisked him when he went to visit The Fixer.

"They're with me," Dixie said, placing an assuring hand on Lady Hebron's shoulder. His peripheral vision caught a "how dare you touch her" expression on Johnson's face as he walked into England's cool evening air. This brought a smile to his face.

"Your cousin said you would pay for our hansom fare," the warehouse sentry said.

Johnson watched Dixie hand the sentry the hansom fare. Then Dixie gave the sentry more money while instructing him to tell the hansom driver to wait. Johnson overheard him tell the sentry he would be returning to the warehouse. Johnson joined Dixie outside the house and was impressed. Dixie was a man who could take charge of a situation. Dixie placed three of the men in strategic positions around the house. When each man had taken his post around Lady Hebron's home, Dixie paid them in advance. Johnson knew that act of faith meant Dixie trusted them and that each man would have a renewed confidence in their assignment. Johnson marveled at Dixie as he smelled each of their breaths to assure they hadn't been drinking before coming. A sleeping sentry could cause a breach in security. Dixie motioned for Johnson to walk with him as he put a fatherly arm around the warehouse sentry and walked him to the hansom. Dixie knew the young man was aware of his reputation as a tough guy in the streets. Johnson was even more impressed with what he heard. "Son I like you. When I came to the warehouse this morning you greeted me with respect and frisked me without being rough or offensive. I like that. That is why I trust you to take back a message to my cousin. It must be delivered in private. If that thug, The Rat, is there say nothing."

The young sentry nodded understanding that Dixie was entrusting him with an important task. One that if done correctly would garner a favor in the future from a well respected thug in England's criminal underworld.

"The Rat was in the room with my cousin this morning and left in a hurry, directly after I mentioned Mr. Johnson. I suspect he played the role of snitch and shared some sensitive information about what my cousin and I talked about, to some pretty mean men," Dixie said. "I took a pretty good beating as a result. You with me so far?"

"I knew it!" The young colored sentry said. "I've been telling your cousin for some time now that The Rat could not be trusted. The Rat did some other things I thought were odd and it hurt your cousin's business. I knew he was behind it but I just couldn't prove it. Your cousin even suspects that The Rat has been conspiring with a rival crime group. They are trying to take our slice of the business away. He can't prove that either but he mentioned it to me. He asked me to watch The Rat carefully."

Johnson and Dixie exchanged glances. It was clear The Fixer was on to The Rat. It was also clear The Fixer trusted the warehouse sentry. Johnson and Dixie also realized the sentry wanted to move up in Dixie's cousin's criminal enterprise. And to do this, the sentry had to prove The Rat could not be trusted. Dixie was convinced the young sentry could be trusted to complete the task. He pulled out more money out and handed it to the young man. "I've already paid for the hansom ride back to the warehouse. But if you have a special young lady in your life, this extra money should help you buy her something real nice. Tell my cousin what The Rat did and what happened as a result. And when this is done I'll go to my cousin personally. I'll speak on your behalf and suggest you be considered as his right hand man. Both you and my cousin need to be careful in dealing with The Rat however. He has too many irons in the fire and you both could get burned."

The young sentry's eyes lit up. "You'll speak to your cousin on my behalf?" the young sentry asked, a gleam of ambition in his eyes.

"I will," Dixie said knowing the boy trusted him. His criminal reputation in the East End streets gave him that credibility. "If he doesn't promote you, I'll steal you from him and you can work for me."

The sentry smiled and wasted no time climbing into the hansom and instructing the driver to hurry back to the warehouse. Johnson and Dixie smiled at one another as the hansom pulled away. The twosome checked to see that each man was positioned in the areas assigned and Dixie verified that each man had his own pistol. He promised each of them he would have Lady Hebron make sandwiches and drinks to hold them through the night.

Johnson and Dixie walked back into the house and made their way to the living room where Lady Hebron was having tea.

Johnson engaged her with light conversation and the two shared some jokes and that resulted in laughter. Johnson noticed Dixie was quiet. He knew Dixie wanted desperately to get to know Lady Hebron. Despite that desire, Dixie remained focused. Altamont had entrusted him to protect Johnson and Lady Hebron whether he actually said it or not. Johnson knew Dixie desperately wanted Altamont to trust him. Johnson knew it was of paramount importance to Dixie that Altamont, and perhaps even Dr. Watson, believed he was a man who could be trusted. Dixie shared the promise he made to the men about sandwiches and drink with Lady Hebron. Upon hearing this, Lady Hebron left immediately for the kitchen to prepare the food. He also asked her to bring him several blankets and a pillow. Johnson realized it was Dixie's intent to sleep in the hallway near the front door. If someone managed to get past the sentries they would get more than their fair share of trouble from Dixie as they entered the door. Johnson smiled at Dixie and admired his serious demeanor. He watched Dixie remove a pistol from the brown paper bag that Johnson thought only contained Dixie's money. Dixie opened the chamber to make sure the gun was fully loaded and then snapped it shut. Johnson shared his observation of Lady Hebron. "She is a nice lady that Lucy Hebron. But I'm afraid after running with the harlots I have for so many years, I'm not sure she will have anything to do with a fellow like me."

"I have no intentions on trying to win her affections either. Altamont is depending on me to keep you and Lady Hebron safe tonight," Dixie said. "I intend on doing just that. I'll be sleeping by the front door in the hallway just to make sure."

Johnson's eyes softened as he looked upon Dixie. "You're a fine man Mr. Dixie. I count it an honor to have met you and been in your company," Johnson said.

Dixie's heart felt great joy with Johnson's words. "Meeting you, Mr. Johnson, was a dream come true for me. I'm afraid my honor in meeting you far exceeds any you may feel," Dixie said.

Dixie then moved to sit in the chair Lady Hebron had vacated next to Johnson. The men sat in silence enjoying the brotherly harmony between them. Lady Hebron emerged from the kitchen with a huge tray full of sandwiches and three pitchers of water. As Dixie left to take the food to the men, Lady Hebron placed blankets and pillows on a chair in the hallway.

"Mr. Dixie you don't have to sleep down here, I have a room that you would be much more comfortable in," Lady Hebron offered.

"Thank you Lady Hebron but trust that I am doing what is best," Dixie said.

Lady Hebron smiled and returned to the living room to finish her tea with Johnson. As Johnson and Lady Hebron talked they heard Dixie return from delivering the food to the guards outside. Dixie put together his makeshift pallet on the floor near the front door and settled in for the night.

"I guess we should all be turning in for the night Mr. Johnson," Lady Hebron said.

"A woman as beautiful as you has no man?" Johnson said.

"I'm not as fortunate as you, Mr. Johnson, to have a companion," Lady Hebron said. "How is your wife by the way?"

Johnson smiled. Lady Hebron's declaration she knew of his wife confirmed he would be sleeping alone. She was a lady for sure and found a nice way to set her boundary with him.

"I'm curious about your travels to the United States and what you thought of my great country," Johnson said, while sipping his tea. He never addressed the reference to his wife.

"I lived in the United States as a child, but I was too young to remember much about it. I suppose it is similar in some regards to England," Lady Hebron said. "Colored people are suffering pretty much the same in either country. You, Mr. Johnson, are quite the hero among coloreds in America, and an absolute hated figure among the whites."

Johnson laughed half-heartedly as he took another sip of tea.

"And quite the ladies man from what I understand," Lady Hebron said. "You're obviously attracted to me but I'm thinking it's because I'm half white. What confuses me is that you only take up with prostitutes. That, Mr. Johnson, I am not."

"No you're not a prostitute and I respect you too much Lady Hebron to even approach you in that manner," Johnson said somberly.

"I appreciate that, Mr. Johnson, because I assure you it would not work. Such a gesture would probably earn you a slap flush against your face," Lady Hebron assured him. "Perhaps two."

Johnson and Lady Hebron giggled together, knowing she would probably make good on her prediction if it came to that.

"Very few people know this about me, Lady Hebron, but

I was married to two colored women at separate times early in my fight career. The marriages were total failures and that is why I only consort with or marry white women," Johnson said. "The first was Mary Austin* in 1898. I loved her deeply and she did some traveling with me but soon the constant travel became too much for her. She simply stopped going with me. The romance fizzled."

Johnson continued. "It was the second marriage to a colored woman that has placed me in my present state of mind about women. Her name was Clara Kerr* and she was a prostitute I met in the summer of 1903 in Philadelphia, Pennsylvania. God knows I loved that woman with all my heart and I gave her the best of everything. We were happy and together for three years until 1906. Can you believe that heifer left me for another man?" Johnson asked Lady Hebron, raising his eyes to meet hers. "To think, all I did for that woman, and she runs off with some racehorse trainer, a friend of mine, no less. When she left she took most of my jewelry and clothing. Even though she betrayed me, I not only missed her company but realized she was one of my greatest loves. I was devastated. I found the two scoundrels in Tucson, Arizona and had him arrested for burglary. She, however, knew I was weak for her. Through seductive persuasion Clara got me back in her bed and soon I forgave her. We moved to California and when I had trouble getting fights, my money ran short, and Clara Kerr left me for good."

Lady Hebron's eyes were welling with tears. "I'm so sorry Mr. Johnson. They ruined you, didn't they?"

"They certainly didn't help, Lady Hebron," Johnson

said. "I tried to have a relationship with colored women, I truly did. But one couldn't handle the lifestyle and the other just wanted to use me for my money and was unfaithful as well. I vowed I would never make myself so vulnerable to any woman of any race for the rest of my life. If it was money they wanted and not me, then I paid them for services rendered. And I will only do this with white women. But from that point on, I never gave and never will give any woman my heart."

Johnson watched Lady Hebron's tears flow down her face feeling the pain he had felt and possibly still felt. He was touched by her compassion. "We should go to bed now. I get the feeling tomorrow is going to be one heck of a day. Good night Lady Hebron."

The two stood and embraced in a hug and made their way to their respective rooms. Dixie feigned sleep as they stepped carefully over him to reach the steps but he had heard every word. His heart was heavy for the embattled colored boxer too.

In the morning, Lady Hebron knocked on Johnson door and informed him breakfast would be ready in one-half hour and made her way down to awaken Dixie but he was already up and sitting quietly in the living room.

"You weren't sleeping last night were you?" Lady Hebron asked him, knowingly.

"No I wasn't," Dixie said.

"Mr. Johnson is going to need our love and support for these next few days," Lady Hebron said. "He is in a foreign land. He has to know he can depend on people of his race."

Dixie nodded in agreement. She left the living room

headed for the kitchen to prepare breakfast. Dixie went outdoors to check on the sentries.

Johnson was already in the living room browsing through an English magazine when Dixie returned to the house. Lady Hebron announce loudly from the kitchen breakfast was being served and brought the hot meal into the living room. The smell invaded both men's nostrils as Lady Hebron stepped into the living room with two breakfast plates piled high with flapjacks, eggs and bacon. Johnson was obviously hungry and began wolfing down his meal. Dixie joined him in the onslaught.

Johnson looked up from his plate long enough to speak.

"Lady Hebron, where did you learn to cook like this? I would swear I'm eating in America," Johnson said.

"Don't forget Mr. Johnson, my father was a colored man from America and this was a meal I watched my mother cook for him," Lady Hebron said as she smiled, satisfied the two the men enjoyed her cooking. It was nice to have men around for a change. As Dixie finished the last bite of eggs on his plate Lady Hebron retreated to the kitchen again, this time emerging with breakfast for the sentries. As Dixie left to feed the men, Johnson leaned back in his chair, rubbing his full belly. Dixie did the same when he returned.

Johnson had shared his life with Lady Hebron so he decided to get an idea what her life was like.

"Lady Hebron I can only imagine what life was like for you being the sibling of a mixed marriage," Johnson said.

Like Johnson, Lady Hebron was not always an open book about her life to friends or strangers. But since Johnson had bore his soul to her the night before, it was only fair to do the same.

"It was a difficult childhood I must admit. My mother Effie lived in Atlanta, Georgia, in America, for a while. She married my father, a colored lawyer. Things were fine until father died during a yellow fever epidemic," Lady Hebron said. "Mother moved back to England and married a white man named Jack Monro. However, mother was too ashamed to tell him I had a black father. As you can see, I carry many of the racial features of my colored father. Mother made me cover myself all the time. I even had to wear a mask to hide my colored features. That was not an easy life to live as a child. My father hired Mr. Holmes to discover the truth. Once he knew, he accepted me as his child. That is how I met Mr. Holmes, or who you refer to as Altamont."

Lady Hebron continued.

"As I grew older, I still had to overcome being ostracized and shunned. As a young adult woman, I decided to pass* myself off as a full blooded white woman. Under that guise, I overcame any prejudice by location change and some deception. And though I had been accepted in what England calls "proper society" while I passed for a white woman, I stayed to myself, read books and learned all I could. My colored father had accumulated some wealth in Atlanta so from his inheritance combined with the inheritance left by my stepfather's, I was able to buy this beautiful Victorian home. Such a home added to my deception of who I truly was. Later, I took a lover, an extremely wealthy colored Brit who was a banker in the East End. I'm ashamed now. He was a married man. I know it was wrong but he gave me money to invest in the stock market and I became wealthy. I guess I'm somewhat of a hypocrite, condemning you for buying women. In essence, this married man used me for my body and I used him for his knowledge of the stock market. I guess that makes me a woman of ill-repute in a way, doesn't it Mr. Johnson?"

"Not at all Lady Hebron," Johnson said. "Did you love him?"

"I did," Lady Hebron answered.

"Then that is what is important," Johnson said.

"I accumulated so much wealth, London's newspapers listed me as one of England's wealthiest women, but they also call me a recluse and they are correct," Lady Hebron said. "Because of my past, I prefer my privacy."

Johnson and Dixie were impressed. But before Lady Hebron could share more, there was a loud roar of a car engine that stopped directly in front of Lady Hebron's home. The sentries voices outside could be heard issuing stern warnings. Soon there were addition voices audible from the yard in response to the sentries. Johnson and Dixie arose and headed to look out the window. Dixie heard his sentries talking with other men outside. Then there was a knock at the front door.

Lady Hebron, out of habit, arose to answer, but Dixie motioned for her to remain seated. He pulled the revolver from his waistband and advanced to the front door quietly.

Dixie peered out the window and there in Lady Hebron's driveway sat an American made Ford Model T*. Two young white men stood at the door and two of the colored sentries stood not to far behind them, pistols drawn, while the third sentry scoured the street visually to confirm there were no more men coming.

Surprisingly, the men didn't look like men at all. They appeared to be teenagers. Johnson opened the door.

"A gentleman named Altamont sent us here. We must admit we had the dickens finding this place. We received a telegram from John Torrio in Chicago on behalf of Diamond Jim Colosimo. We were conducting some business in Ireland, but Mr. Torrio instructed us to get to England as soon as possible. He said a friend of his needed help. We're here to meet with Mr. Jack Johnson," the oldest of the two teenagers said.

"Oh, do come in," Johnson said. He glanced at the car the two Americans arrived in. Just like Americans to make a loud and grand entrance, he thought to himself. Johnson led the teenagers to the living room. Meanwhile Dixie thanked the sentries for escorting the teenagers to the door and sent them back to their positions. As Dixie entered the living room, Johnson was surveying the teenagers before introducing himself.

"My name is Jack Johnson," he said, shaking both of their hands. "I must admit, I thought Mr. Torrio would send someone older but you must obviously be 'capable' men."

"We are very capable, Mr. Johnson. Mr. Torrio wouldn't have sent us had we had not been. My name is Frankie Yale* out of New York," Yale said.

"And I'm Capone, Alphonse Capone*," the youngest teenager said. "You can call me Al though. It's a real pleasure to meet you Mr. Johnson." The youthful glee was apparent in his voice.

The chubby Yale was of medium height and his fists

were scarred slightly. From experience in the fight business, Johnson realized Yale had engaged in a few fistfights in his day. Johnson estimated Yale couldn't be more that 18-years-old.

The Capone kid was the curious one to Johnson however. The kid had the look of a killer in his eyes, or if he hadn't killed anyone, his eyes said he was capable of and would eventually kill. Johnson estimated Al Capone to be about 14-years-old. Capone had a grotesque scar* on his face. A scar Johnson believed was no more than a year old at best.

They both had heavy Italian accents. Johnson could tell by the look in Dixie's eyes that he realized the telegram Johnson sent to Colosimo was a request for Italian Mafia protection. If Johnson was going to deal with danger in England, he was going to do so with the aid of American's crime syndicate. Capone and Yale were Colosimo's response to Johnson's request.

Again there was a knock at the door and Johnson followed Dixie who went to the hallway window to look outside again. They saw the young colored sentry. Johnson told Dixie to open the door. The sentry had two more colored Brits with him.

"I delivered the message privately to your cousin as you instructed," the young man said. "He sent me back with these men to relieve the sentries sent last night. He said you would pay for the hansom."

"Take care of this Mr. Dixie, I have to go back in and talk with Mr. Yale and Capone," Johnson said.

"Indeed I will," Dixie replied. Dixie paid the hansom driver for round trip expenses and thanked the three overnight sentries and again gave each some bonus pay and watched them pull off. He walked with the new sentries to the tool shed behind the huge estate. It was open and he found some tools. He gave each man a task to do in the yard. There was much work to be done to the property surrounding the house. While Lady Hebron kept the interior of her home in immaculate condition, the landscape outside needed attending. Dixie thought this would be a good cover. If any nosy neighbors were to pass they would see colored men doing landscape work and think nothing of it. But in reality each one was armed and dangerous and primed to protect those inside.

With Dixie now having his security team in place on the outside, he was more interested in getting back inside the house and finding out about Johnson new, personal security team. With The Fixer's guys on the outside and Johnson's American gangsters on the inside, the property was more than safe. Once inside, Dixie saw that Lady Hebron had prepared Yale and Capone breakfast. As they concluded their meal Johnson was trying to satisfy his curiosity.

"How did you get here so quickly?" Johnson asked.

"As I said, Alphonse and I were in Ireland conducting some business for our friends in New York," Frankie Yale said. "Lucky for you, Mr. Johnson, our friends in New York had a Model T Ford transported to Ireland for our use. The transportation system we heard was less than desirable in Ireland. Mr. Colosimo knew you were in a pinch and needed us here as fast as possible. Alphonse and I paid two Irish gentlemen to drive us here. We left yesterday afternoon and traveled all night to arrive just this morning. We paid for the men to travel back to Ireland by some other means. Chicago seems to think a great deal of you, Mr. Johnson, to dispatch Alphonse and me so quickly, and by God's grace we happened to be close enough to oblige."

"And I think a great deal of them as well," Johnson said.

Another knock at the door and Lucy, with Dixie behind her, went to answer. It was Altamont and Dr. Watson. Lucy showed them to the living room.

"Well, I see you found your way," Altamont said as he shook Yale's hand. Dr. Watson seemed totally uncomfortable with the room full of strangers and moved to a sitting chair where he had clear view of everyone.

"We did, Mr. Holmes, and the London countryside reminds me somewhat of Italy," Yale said.

"I would hope that was a compliment," Dr. Watson said with a tone of sarcasm.

"Show some respect old man," Capone snapped in an intimidating voice. "We're on your side."

"You're on Mr. Johnson's side, young man," Dr. Watson quipped. "I don't know of you, didn't send for you, and not sure I want to know much about you."

"Why you wise-assed Brit," Capone said, making a move towards Dr. Watson. Yale placed his hand on Capone, restraining him.

"Wise move I say," Dr. Watson said, pulling his gun out and placing it on his lap.

It was clear Dr. Watson did not think much of the New York mobsters. But a characteristic became clear about Capone: he had a quick temper.

"I had a very nice conversation with the two Irish gentlemen who drove you here, Mr. Yale. I know them as well.

When I was in Buffalo, New York it became apparent that some factions in New York City had dealings with Irish friends of mine," Altamont said, moving to the center of the floor to gain control of the room. "But never mind that. We have very little time to close this situation and like it or not, we all have to cooperate as a team."

Altamont looked squarely at Dixie.

"Mr. Dixie that was a pure stroke of genius putting the sentries to work as landscapers. It certainly is the perfect cover for them. Each day you surprise me. Job well done," Altamont said. "I also believe I've found the gentleman who has been leaking information about everyone's whereabouts. I suggest Mr. Dixie, Mr. Yale and Mr. Capone pay him a visit. However it is best you leave that loud gaudy American car behind. It would bring to much attention on you and in this instance we all must move with as much stealth as possible. In fact I'll have the car moved to the back of the house so not to draw any unwarranted attention. Here is the name of the pub you'll find him in." Altamont walked the threesome to the door to give them final instructions. He had the hansom awaiting them and watched as they sped off to their mission.

"What a sordid bunch I find myself associated with this day," Altamont could hear Dr. Watson say as he entered the living room. Watson was always the more conservative of the two. His being considered a "man of proper society," the doctor's first choice would not be to associate with colored thugs and American gangsters. But Altamont also knew Watson would have his back.

Chapter 8

Dixie was not enthusiastic about being sent into the streets of East London with two youths from New York. But he had to trust that Altamont knew what he was doing. The teenagers looked out the windows of the hansom like grade school kids on a field trip. Their lack of maturity concerned him. Could they handle themselves if trouble erupted? They told him they did not bring weapons to London and that Torrio in his telegram had said their "dates" would be provided by Johnson. Johnson, before the three left Lady Hebron's, asked Dixie to find Yale and Capone guns. Dixie assured Johnson he could purchase weapons after Johnson explained the term "dates" meant firearms. No good mafia man ever appeared in public without a date. Dixie knew a guy at the bar where they were headed, who, for the right price, could accommodate him.

Altamont paid the hansom driver a liberal amount of cash to not only take the three ruffians to the bar but to also wait for them as they went in to complete their mission. The hansom driver actually whistled after counting the payment. "For these wages dear chap, I'm at your service for the rest of the day," he told Altamont.

Yale remarked to Dixie there was a distinct scenery drop-off as they left West London. They arrived at the seedy side of East London where the pub was located. Johnson described Capone, to Dixie, as what Americans called "young and full of piss and vinegar." Dixie understood what Johnson meant as he watched Capone whistle and wave to prostitutes on the corners as they drove into the East End. Capone had to be reminded by Yale they were in England on business. Dixie also took that opportunity to remind them they must keep a low profile. They arrived at the pub and instructed the hansom driver to await them, a distance from the pub, but within eye sight.

As they entered the pub, Yale and Capone broke out in smiles. "Kind of remind you of the Harvard Inn*, doesn't it Alphonse?" Yale said with a smile.

"Sure does," Capone replied.

They sat at a table near the door. Every eye in the pub seemed to be trained on them. A colored man with a criminal reputation such as Dixie's, in the company of two white Americans, was enough to draw attention. Dixie ignored them as he scanned the room and spotted MacGregor seated towards the back of the pub. McGregor sat with his back to the wall while puffing furiously on a cigarette. McGregor nodded his head to acknowledge Dixie. MacGregor was of Scottish descent and specialized in the sale of handguns. Often the merchandise he sold were stolen firearms of the black market variety. Dixie left Yale and Capone at the table and walked to McGregor's table. Dixie whispered in his ear that he was in need of firearms and MacGregor beckoned for Dixie to follow him out of the back entrance. Once outside, in the alley, in back of the bar, Dixie chose two American made Colt snub-nosed revolvers. "I'll even throw in some free ammunition," McGregor said.

Dixie didn't know how McGregor was able to get firearms from all over the world. But on this occasion, with McGregor having seen Dixie enter the bar with the Americans, the snub-nosed revolvers would be an easy sale to Dixie. Dixie handed McGregor payment and walked nonchalantly back into the pub.

Under the table, Dixie handed Yale and Capone the revolvers and a box of ammunition each. Yale whistled, obviously impressed. "I was prepared to use my fist if needed be, but my friend, this certainly makes me feel a bit more at home," Yale said. He slid his revolver to Capone.

"Alphonse, go the bathroom and get these "ladies" ready in case we run into a prom date," Yale said coolly. Capone smiled and made his way to the bathroom.

"Did you get one for yourself?" Yale asked, looking Dixie square in the eyes.

"No. I have a pistol back at Lady Hebron but I really prefer to use the knife as my first line of defense," Dixie said dryly. "I figure if there is some chap close enough for me to slit his guts open, he probably didn't mean me any good. That my friend is defensible in a court of law."

"I hear you my friend," Yale replied. "But in my line of business, in New York, when we shoot someone, we don't leave any witnesses, so a court of law isn't a consideration."

As Yale said that, Capone returned, slid Yale his snub-nosed revolved, and smiled sheepishly.

"The "ladies" are ready to dance," Capone said.

"Who are we looking for, anyway?" Yale asked coolly.

"Him," Dixie replied, as a dirty, skinny looking white Brit entered the pub. "They call him The Weasel."

"I see why," Capone snickered. "He looks like one for sure." Yale motioned to Capone and Capone got up and walked to position himself near the door.

"Handle your business, Mr. Dixie," Yale said as he placed his snubbed-nose revolver in his lap. "Alphonse and I have got your back."

Dixie nodded. He was nervous on how all of this was going to go down. Dixie walked to the bar where The Weasel had just been served a beer by the bartender. Dixie still wasn't sure if he could rely on the teenagers if things got hairy but he had handled such situations alone and survived. He would get through this one too. The Weasel looked up, startled, as he realized Dixie towered over his shoulder.

"Someone wants to see you Weasel," Dixie said. After hesitating for just a moment, The Weasel lifted his mug and threw his beer in Dixie's face as he bolted towards the door. There was a rush of activity based on The Weasel's action as some men seated at the tables stood up, probably coming to The Weasel's aid.

Yale pushed his table over violently and raised his snubbed-nosed revolver in the direction of the responding men.

"Be cool my friends, be cool," Yale said as he pointed his weapon at them. "This is business that has nothing to do with you. Have a seat." The men shot angry glares at Yale but he had the jump on them, so they took their seats.

At that same moment The Weasel was just a few feet away from the door, apparently thinking he had escaped. That was until Capone threw a cold-cocked punch directly into The Weasel's nose. The punch could be heard throughout the bar. The Weasel crumpled to the floor. Capone's wicked punch had laid The Weasel out on the floor, unconscious. Dixie walked over and with the help of Capone began dragging The Weasel out of the pub's front door. By now, Yale had made his way to the front door snub-nosed revolver cocked and loaded in full view of everyone in the bar. Yale stood at the pub's front door entrance, covering Dixie and Capone with his weapon, while they dragged The Weasel out on the street. Yale backed out of the bar and stood just yards from the entrance, gun aimed at the entrance. Some men tried to follow from the bar, onto the street, but they retreated back into the pub upon seeing Yale's snub-nosed revolver still at the ready. Capone whistled for the hansom driver who pulled up hurriedly. He and Dixie loaded the unconscious man in the hansom. Yale backed up to the hansom, gun still trained on the bar's entrance, and climbed in. The hansom driver cried out to his horses and drove off in a fury.

Once the escape was successful and he knew no one was in pursuit, Yale smiled at Dixie and spoke. "So much for keeping a low profile," he said, laughing heartily.

The ride back to Lady Hebron's home was uneventful and The Weasel was dumped on a couch in a back room of Lady Hebron's house when they arrived. The smelling salt Dr. Watson administered to The Weasel brought him back to consciousness. As the cobwebs cleared from his head, his vision became clear, and he saw Altamont seated in a smoking chair positioned at his side. Dr. Watson moved away from him as he peered frightened about the room. He jumped slightly as he locked gazes with Capone who had an amused smile on his face.

"Why did you run Mr. Weasel? My friends were there in peace, they weren't there to harm you," Altamont assured him.

"You could have fooled me," The Weasel replied, rubbing his nose where Capone had clocked him. "All I know is that the colored chap Dixie moves in some really shady circles and when he told me someone wanted to see me I was thinking I was going for a one way ride."

"Well that's how it usually goes in America," Yale said, as he and Capone chuckled at their inside joke. Back in New York, when someone crossed the Mafia, that person would be placed in a car and taken to a desolated area and killed.

The Weasel's demeanor brightened some as the lovely Lady Hebron handed him a cup of tea. "I could probably use something a bit stronger, madam, but this will do for a start," The Weasel said, smiling at Lucy. "So why am I here?"

"You are a snitch, my slimy, weasel friend, and you almost got our associate, Mr. Dixie, seriously hurt," Capone said.

"Very true Mr. Weasel," Altamont said. "You made it your business to fall in league with two gentlemen from South Africa. Their intentions, we have yet to determine. We understand you shared information about Mr. Johnson's whereabouts. Your reputation tells me you did this for financial gain. Correct?"

The Weasel nodded his head.

"So what do they want with Mr. Johnson, my dear friend?" Altamont asked.

"I honestly don't know," The Weasel said.

Capone stood up, walked to The Weasel, grabbing him with both hands by the collar, pulling their faces within inches of one another.

"Don't know or won't say?" Capone yelled in The Weasel's face.

At that moment Dr. Watson let out a loud exclamation, "Oh my God."

The Weasel had urinated on himself.

"What a wimp," Capone said as he released The Weasel, shoving him back onto the couch. "Lady Hebron, you might want to excuse yourself. This man just pissed on himself."

"Can I be excused to clean up?" The Weasel asked Altamont. His face was flushed with embarrassment.

"When we're finished," Altamont replied. Capone, Yale, Johnson and Dixie couldn't help but snicker at the pitiful little man as he sat on the couch with the front of his trousers soaked in his own urine. "You're going to play a key role tonight. In a real life stage performance, to be played out on the streets of the lower East End, my wet friend. After we find you a change of clothes and get you cleaned up, you're going to find your two South African cronies and tell them you have knowledge that Mr. Johnson will be in the lower East End tonight. Convince them you will be involved in leading a good, old fashioned American style lynching party, with Mr. Johnson as the guest of honor."

"What?" Johnson asked, with a loud voice of surprise combined with protest. "You've got to be kidding me! Ain't nobody putting a rope around my neck. They haven't tried in America and I'll be damn if I'm gonna let a bunch of Brits have the privilege."

"Relax, Mr. Johnson," Altamont said, still keeping his eyes trained on The Weasel. "Remember I sent a telegram to Harry Houdini?"

"I do," Johnson replied.

"Well he responded," Altamont said. "Houdini, as you well know, is the world's greatest illusionist, and he sent me his secret to an illusion I saw him perform. He hung himself by the neck, by a rope, and walked away very much alive. Will you entrust your life to me Mr. Johnson? You saved me in America so I owe you the same courtesy."

"I don't like it, but since you put it that way, I have no choice," Johnson said.

"Good. It is settled then," Altamont said, standing to his feet. "Let's get you ready Mr. Weasel and I'll get word to my B Street Irregulars that the plan is a go."

"All you need do is inform your South African friends of the lynching party and lead them to it, and actually participate, to add validity to our little charade," Altamont said.

"I've got to see this," Yale said. "The boys back in New York will never believe it."

"You, Mr. Yale and Mr. Capone will accompany The Weasel to the meeting with the South Africans, posing as irate Americans who want to see Mr. Johnson lynched. South Africa is a racist society based on many of the principles held in such high esteem in America," Altamont said. "It should be an easy sale, if you do it correctly."

"This just gets better by the minute," Yale said, then turning to Johnson. "Don't get me wrong, Mr. Johnson. I'm not excited about the prospect of lynching you. But just the idea of pulling this thing off is exciting."

"There are folks in America, Mr. Yale, who would pay good money for the perceived task you are about to undertake," Johnson said, with a sad smile.

Yale produced some clothing for The Weasel while assuring the ruffian he did not have to return them. Altamont then briefed The Weasel on what his role in the plan was. He also reminded him he could not rescue him from Yale or Capone's wrath if he failed to do exactly as instructed.

The Weasel nodded. Capone had instilled fear in the man's heart.

The game was afoot. The plan now in play!

Chapter 9

Johnson and Altamont watched Capone, Yale and The Weasel leave in the hansom. The twosome returned to the living room.

"I must excuse myself, gentlemen," Altamont said. "I have to prepare a solution that is essential for tonight's lynching. Lady Hebron, do you have a work space I can use? I have all the chemicals I need."

"I'll show you the perfect area, Mr. Holmes," Lady Hebron said. "After that I'll get some dinner started. I know the men are hungry. It is so nice to have company."

Lady Hebron and Altamont left the living room leaving Dixie, Johnson and Dr. Watson seated in the living room.

"Now that we have a moment Mr. Johnson, can I be frank with you?" Dr. Watson asked.

"By all means, Dr. Watson," Johnson replied. "Not only can you be Frank with me, you can be Earnest as well."

Dixie shook his head at the pun.

"Your promiscuous shenanigans with white women in the eyes of the American public are wrong. Do you honestly believe what you are doing is right and acceptable?" Dr. Watson asked.

"I will admit Dr. Watson; there is a campaign of hatred and bigotry that has been waged against me by whites who wish to regain the heavyweight title and they use my relationship with white women to fuel that initiative," Johnson said. "Like you, they are prejudice, and refuse to look at the human right a man and woman have to engage in a relationship, no matter their skin color."

"Whoa there Mr. Johnson, how dare you call me prejudice," Dr. Watson said. "Mr. Dixie do you share a similar sentiment as Mr. Johnson?"

"I respectfully ask not to comment," Dixie said. "This conversation is between you and Mr. Johnson."

Dr. Watson realized this might be a silent affirmation on Dixie's behalf. Nonetheless he pressed on.

"Let's be honest, Mr. Johnson. It is said the white women who you consort with are prostitutes, am I right?" Dr Watson asked.

"Yes, they are mostly prostitutes. My money helps them to maintain a living," Johnson said.

"Your response is unbelievable, Mr. Johnson," Dr. Watson said. "You are paying these women to defile themselves for your perverted pleasure. I can only imagine the gross desires you have. It sickens me to even think about it."

Johnson, with a tone of indignation in his voice, responded. "How dare you question me, Dr. Watson, and call me perverted. I don't hear you calling white men in your social circle, who we both know, pay for the company of prostitutes, to do with them whatever, perverts. I tire of people like you and your double standards. White men, heck men in general for that matter, have been paying for sexual favors for centuries. Certainly long before me. What say you of them my fine doctor? I'm sure you know of white men who you associate with in your esteemed social circle that pay good money for a toss in the hay with a whore. Do you call them out on their "shenanigans"? I doubt it seriously."

"I am a married man who holds true to my marital

vows," Dr. Watson said. "I make it a habit to consort with men of my station who do the same."

"Do you approach white men of your station who you know who don't? Who sleep with whores? Do you approach them the same way you just approached me?" Johnson asked again, this time more forceful.

"No," Dr. Watson answered slowly. Johnson was taken back for moment with Dr. Watson's honesty.

"Then why did you single my indiscretions out? Why, because I'm colored? Because it pains you to know neither you nor any white man within thousands of miles can knock me down let alone out? Does that make your race feel inferior?" Johnson said, this time increasing the volume of his voice. "Does it make you mad that a colored man has more money at his disposal than you Dr. Watson? Does it make you mad that perhaps a white woman would desire the feel of my dark body next to her on a regular basis as opposed to that of a white man?"

Johnson stopped there and abruptly left the living room, walking outdoors to compose his temper. Dr. Watson looked at Dixie. Dixie stood and left the room as well. Dr. Watson sat silently alone with his thoughts.

Lady Hebron could hear the entire conversation from the room where Sherlock was setting up chemicals to prepare his solution. When the conversation between Johnson and Dr. Watson seemed to get heated, Lady Hebron was about to go to the living room to intercede. Altamont placed his hand gently on her shoulder to restrain her from going.

"Those two need this, they need to have this

conversation," Altamont told her. Now that it appeared that Johnson had walked outside, Altamont nodded his head, in affirmation to Lady Hebron, that maybe this was the appropriate moment to go.

When she walked in the living room she found Dr. Watson sitting alone in thought. "That didn't go as well as you hoped?" Lady Hebron asked.

"I'm afraid maybe the way I approached Mr. Johnson was a bit too much," Dr. Watson said. "He accused me of being prejudice and he asked some really good questions. Why approach only him in regards to relations with prostitutes? Surely, I can name a handful of my white colleagues who pay for prostitutes' services. I don't feel the need to confront them. Am I prejudiced?"

Lady Hebron had been a victim of prejudice in her lifetime but she probably had not seen the racism at such a level as Jack Johnson. She understood the time and era in which colored people lived.

"Dr. Watson, you are merely a man of the time in which we live. You simply mirror the attitude of whites so prevalent in both England and America," Lady Hebron said. "The question you have to ask yourself is whether your indignation towards Mr. Johnson is singular and because he's colored, or because you resent men buying prostitutes in general. In your mind, is this a morally wrong practice, or is it deeper? Is it that a colored man is buying white prostitutes? Is it that according to our society, as it exist today, colored men buying white prostitutes is the real sin or is this practice an abomination within our society as a whole? It seems to me, you are battling two issues within your conscience. Mr. Johnson shared with me last night that he did indeed marry colored women in his early years but had his heart broken. One stole from him, and was unfaithful. When he forgave that woman, and tried to work the relationship out, she still left him because he didn't have the money to keep her in the lifestyle she wanted," Lady Hebron said. "The man is deeply scarred from that experience, Dr. Watson. Whether the way he is now responding is right or wrong I cannot say, for this certainly is a matter of the heart. His taking up with white prostitutes serves two acts of his own personal rebellion: one against black women because he no longer trusts them and perhaps the second simply to thumb his nose at the racist society in which he lives. He is the epitome of an expression I heard my colored father say many times, that 'He is cutting his nose off to spite his face'. "

The expression on Dr. Watson's face had softened considerably. He never knew of Johnson's previous heartache.

"In the matter of prejudice I certainly am not in a position to judge that," Lady Hebron said. "My mother made me cover myself and wear a mask to hide my colored features. I have the blood of a colored man coursing through my veins and I wonder if you would have a less positive opinion of me if I did not have this home and great wealth?"

Before Dr. Watson could speak they could hear the front door open. Johnson entered the living room.

"I owe you an apology Dr. Watson," Johnson said walking to Dr. Watson as he extended his arm to shake hands. Dr. Watson extended his hand to accept Johnson's. "Every time I meet someone, my relationship with white women is always the first question. No one wants to know how I feel, what my life's goals are, they ask nothing but why I do what I do? You have to understand the American society, Dr. Watson. There are poor white people and immigrants in America who are treated just as poorly as colored people. America is the land of haves and have-nots. The white American male has had his ego bruised to think a white woman would dare bed down with a colored man and they rationalize that any white woman who would do such a thing had to be a prostitute. That if I wasn't buying their affection, they would not be with me of their own will. Perhaps they are right. No white American woman of 'proper society' has ever accepted my invitation to dinner or to the opera. They know that one date with me would ruin their lives forever."

Johnson continued. "When I won the heavyweight title there was a ripple of disbelief and that was the beginning of ill-will towards me. In early April of 1909 it became public knowledge I was involved with Belle Schreiber* and days later on April 19, Jim Jeffries, America's great white champion, decided to come out of retirement. I'm sure they wanted him to beat me senseless for consorting with Belle. Things got worst when in October of the same year I took up with Etta Duryea and by then there was talk of legislation being formed specifically to stop me from being with white women. That legislation was passed and now I am here in England, a fugitive on the run from my own country."

"I read about that," Dr. Watson said. "They called it the "White Slavery Traffic Act.*"

"The American press calls it the Mann Act. In June of 1910, President William Taft signed off on the bill that said any man crossing state lines for the purpose of prostitution or what they called immoral purposes was in violation of the law," Johnson said. "I was set up for a conviction because any white woman I bedded down was called a prostitute. I married Etta* in 1911 but it didn't make a difference. In the eyes of God I had done right by her but man's law said I was a criminal. I was convicted not for breaking the Mann Act after it was passed. I was convicted based on taking a woman across state lines before the law was passed. A relationship and trip that happened two years before the Mann Act was enacted. That is pure prejudice and a gross misinterpretation of the law to convict me based on actions before a law was passed!"

"Well it's not my place to judge whether the law is justified or not is it, Mr. Johnson, but I will say it is highly irregular to convict someone on new legislation with a past violation," Dr. Watson said.

"Convenient how you will not judge white man's laws but you have no problem casting judgment on me and my character, Dr. Watson," Johnson said.

"Come, come my dear man. I'm not judging you but I'm looking at how an interracial relationship will affect a child who has to grow up in this society," Dr. Watson said. "Our dear Lady Hebron has been emotionally scarred however for being the innocent sibling of a mixed marriage."

"I have no children and plan not to have children," Johnson said. "That sir is a moot argument in my case."

"But if society turns a blind eye to you and a relationship with a white woman, others will follow your lead. They will have children and their children will never be accepted in society, they will be ostracized, and ultimately may never be able to fully contribute to society," Dr. Watson said. "Proper society will never accept a half-breed child."

It was then Dr. Watson cringed, remembering Lucy Hebron was seated in the room. She spoke.

"Yes, Dr. Watson you're right … a 'half breed child' as you call me will have a difficult time in society as we know it now," Lucy said.

The embarrassment was apparent in Dr. Watson's voice.

"Lady Hebron, please forgive me. I meant you no harm with that statement. You are a fine woman, kind, compassionate and well-spoken," Dr. Watson said.

"My point exactly," Lady Hebron said. "I am educated, and I have contributed to society, despite the blatant racism I've experienced. You just sat there yourself, Dr. Watson, and said I'm a good person. That means you have gotten to know me. Your opinion of me is formed despite the fact my father is colored and mother white. Don't you realize as the years advance, when more colored people become educated, an opinion such as yours will fall on deaf ears. You have to face the fact, Dr. Watson, that folks with opinions like yours will soon be a dying breed."

"What do you think Mr. Dixie?" Lucy Hebron asked as Dixie, who was now rejoining the group in the living room.

"I doubt seriously Dr. Watson wants to hear the opinion of an admitted rogue, grifter, intimidator and thief," Dixie said. "But I think I'm a bit more progressive in thought regarding the issue of race. Maybe not now, but with the turn of a new century, this discussion will no longer be an issue. I happen to believe that by the turn of the century, England could have a colored Prime Minister or America a colored president*."

Dixie continued. "Dr. Watson, you keep a list of wrongs against me but there are British whites from what you call 'proper society' who have hired me to rough up some undesirable men in hopes of persuading him to stop pursuing their daughters. When it comes to that I am perfectly welcomed in their homes. Because they embrace my criminal element. But when it's time to find defenders, when my reputation is being disparaged, those same 'proper society' folks who hired me turn their backs on me and remain silent as if they never knew me. Too ashamed to admit I sat in their parlors and sipped tea with them as they commissioned me to do their dirty work. I question 'proper society' and its true definition."

"Exactly," Johnson chimed in. "The same promoters who rake in tons of cash by sponsoring my fights are the same people seemingly indignant with my consorting with white women. I'm good enough to make them money, but not good enough for their women."

Dixie continued. "And while I respect Mr. Johnson, and his right to take up with any woman, I prefer relationships with women of my race. But somehow, there is still some reason for 'proper society' to hate me. Colored people are damn if we do, and damn if we don't. There will always be some reason for whites to dislike colored people in my estimation."

Altamont entered the room, apparently finished mixing his solution, and asked, "Might I interject? What I thought was most interesting was Mr. Johnson's victory over Jim Jeffries on America's Independence Day in 1910. When Mr. Johnson defeated Jeffries, there were riots* throughout America. Riots that resulted in people dying. I would assume whites in that country were retaliating at ordinary colored people for Jeffries loss. Surprisingly, the colored people fought back because some whites lost their lives as well. Either way you look at it, Mr. Johnson has empowered an entire race of people, and that is what white America fears the most. Sadly, the debate of which you three have embarked will not be solved here. It will not be solved anytime soon. I would imagine when we are long in our graves, even into the next century, race relations will be a topic of great debate."

"You may have a point," Dr. Watson said.

"I agree," Johnson said.

"Well one thing is certain," Altamont said. "If we go into tonight's adventure a divided front, we place ourselves in grave danger. We have no idea what our South African friends are capable of, especially when their backs are against the wall. We also have to factor in we have an unidentified assassin with Mr. Johnson in his crosshairs. This night, we must be a united front, no matter our skin color."

Altamont knew the danger of his plan that he and his cohorts were about to embark on. It was essential he have Dr. Watson, Johnson, Dixie and Lady Hebron on the same page. Whether they were aware or not, the game was afoot and a dangerous one it would be as his plan progressed.

Chapter 10

The Weasel knocked on the door. Kessler opened it slightly, to peer out, a security chain, designed to reinforce the door, dangled just below his chin. He looked at The Weasel and then eyed Capone and Yale suspiciously. He seemed reluctant to let the threesome in. The quiet click of a pistol's trigger being pulled back could be heard ever so slightly.

"Who are these people?" Kessler asked.

"Friends from America, they are going to provide a great service for you, if you let us in to explain," The Weasel said. Kessler stepped back to allow the door to open, his weapon fully visible.

Capone pulled back his jacket as they entered and coolly pulled back the trigger of his snub-nosed revolver.

"Yours have bullets, my friend? Mine does too," Capone said. "We need your help, not a shoot out!"

"Now, now, buddy we are here as allies. Put that away," Yale said to Capone. Capone closed the hammer of his gun. Yale and Capone were playing the "good cop, bad cop" routine that they witnessed so often when detectives questioned them. It worked. Kessler closed his gun hammer. Wilson walked up to join the group.

"These gentlemen are from America and they have it on good authority that Jack Johnson is going to be in the lower East End tonight," The Weasel said. "They have paid a group of Brits to help them capture Johnson. Tonight they're going to hang him, just like they would in America. Any problem with that?"

Wilson eyed the two Americans.

"I don't give a damn about some *kaffer* being hung by

the neck," Kessler said as he reached in his pocket. He handed The Weasel an American fifty dollar bill. "I just want you to get his keys and bring them to me." The Weasel pocketed the money and nodded his head.

"Getting the keys is not a problem but it will be best if you and Mr. Wilson are in attendance. That way you get the keys immediately," The Weasel said.

"And what would be the names of you two Yanks?" Kessler asked.

"We're about to hang a colored man in a country that is foreign to us my friend," Yale said. "We don't have a name, and as far as we are concerned, neither do you. So let us keep it at that. However, you've greased that gentleman's palm with cash, but my friend and I are making the whole thing possible," Yale said. Wilson handed a fifty dollar bill to Yale.

"When do we go?" Wilson asked.

"Now," Capone said. He grabbed The Weasel by the arm heading out the door, Yale followed close behind.

"Grab my coat," Kessler told Wilson, as he pursued the threesome. He had just laid out some cash and wanted to make sure he got his money's worth. The men all loaded in the hansom Yale had waiting. The ride to the East End street where the lynching was to take place was short. The Weasel instructed the driver to stop at an alley connected to a street where a loud roar could be heard.

"Hurry through this alley," Yale said with urgency, after paying the driver more fare than needed while instructing him to stay, telling the driver his two friends would need a ride to another location. As they rushed into the alley, the two South

Africans failed to see the hansom waiting a block away. Dr. Watson and Dixie sat calmly within it, watching the South Africans. Altamont's plot was unfolding.

As the five men entered the street adjoining the alley, the scene was pandemonium. Three men had three ropes around Johnson's upper torso with his arms entrapped within.

"You gents weren't lying," Kessler said as he watched the hapless Johnson being led to a sturdy lamppost. Altamont, in yet another disguise, stood on a stepladder next to the lamppost, a rope knotted with skill into a noose, dangling at the end.

Yale whispered to Capone. "This is so real." Unbeknownst to Yale, perhaps he, and even Capone, had grown attached to the colored man they were sent to protect. The fear in Johnson's eyes was real. Yale almost wanted to pull his snub-nosed revolver and save Johnson, but he trusted Altamont, so he stayed true to script.

"Okay, you two stay in the shadows," Yale said as he handed Kessler his revolver. "I'll stay with you, as your prisoner if you will, until they hang him, and The Weasel returns with the keys."

Kessler and Wilson nodded respecting that Yale had voluntarily become their hostage. They stayed hidden in the shadows with Yale. Capone and The Weasel walked over to join the crowd. As they neared the scene, the stench of men seeking death was thick, convincing. Capone made his way to the noose and beckoned for the three men holding Johnson captive with the ropes to come to him. Capone fitted the noose around Johnson's neck exactly as Altamont had instructed. Altamont tied the other end of the rope to a hansom and instructed the driver to pull forward.

Johnson's huge body was lifted to the very top of the lamppost and per Altamont's instruction he kicked his legs violently, and then went still. It was easy to do for Johnson, since he had witnessed a hanging as a child in Texas. He kept his eyes closed and didn't move. Because he was so high, and because of the darkness and distance from the shadow of the alley, where Kessler and Wilson were hidden, the best they could tell, Johnson was dead.

The Weasel and some men in the lynching party laid hold to Johnson's possessions. Capone lifted the keys above his head and stood in front of the lynch mob, who were still excited from witnessing a man's death.

"I'm selling this dead man's possessions," Capone said loudly. "I'll start with his keys. Any buyers?"

"Fifty American dollars for the dead man's keys," The Weasel said, true to script.

"They're yours my friend," Capone said. He went to The Weasel and collected the cash.

"I get my money back, right?" 'The Weasel whispered.

"In your dreams," Capone whispered back. The Weasel cursed Capone under his breath, knowing he was out fifty dollars. He had to leave though and had no time to argue with Capone. The Weasel, still miffed about losing money to Capone, ran to the three figures in the alley. He handed the keys to Kessler.

"Okay, lets get out of here, we got what we came for," Kessler exclaimed with glee. He handed Yale his revolver and made haste behind Wilson to the waiting hansom. Yale followed them to confirm they left and then he returned to the street.

"They are gone," Yale hollered.

Altamont cut the rope attached to the hansom and four of the B Street Irregulars caught Johnson as his body dropped from the lamppost. The faces of the men who were present, and weren't aware of Altamont's lynching illusion, showed surprised and fear as Johnson removed the noose, very much alive. Altamont handed The Weasel a wad of cash and the fifty dollars Capone hustled from him.

"I suggest you pay each man correctly because they each know how much they should receive and if you come up short with any of them, we might just see you dangling from that lamppost in the morning," Altamont told The Weasel. The Weasel nodded acknowledging he understood the warning. Altamont, Johnson and the two New York mobsters jumped into a hansom they had waiting while they conducted the lynching. Altamont instructed the driver to go one street over. The hansom, with Dr. Watson and Dixie was gone, but Dr. Watson held up his end of the plan. Dr. Watson dripped the solution on the ground that Altamont had concocted earlier that day. It was phosphorus in nature, and glowed brightly on the dark road. Dr. Watson and Dixie's hansom was following the route of the hansom the two South Africans. Dr. Watson was leaving a trail of Altamont's mystery solution so Altamont's hansom could follow.

"My version of chemical breadcrumbs," Altamont said proudly. "The game is afoot Mr. Johnson. Follow those glowing drippings, driver."

"I think I read that 'the game is afoot' saying in one of

the Sherlock Holmes adventures,*" Capone said showing a childish glee. "This is way too cool."

"You read Sherlock Holmes adventures?" Yale asked in an astounded tone.

"Don't tell the guys when we get back to New York," Capone begged Yale.

"Didn't you get fifty bucks from The Weasel for the keys? That will buy my silence," Yale said slyly.

"You crook," Capone said to Yale as he forked over the $50 bill.

"This never happened and thank you for the compliment," Yale said as he pushed the bill into his breast shirt pocket.

"Unbelievable," Capone said with mock disgust. "And this guy is my friend, the man who covers my back."

"The hustler just got hustled," Altamont said.

Everyone one in the hansom laughed, even Capone. But as Capone laughed he glanced at Altamont, and something dawned on him after hearing Altamont's 'game is afoot' statement: he realized he was in league with the great Sherlock Holmes. Chills ran through his body. The man's reputation for locking up bad guys was legendary. Since he and Yale were on Altamont's side, it was his hope the great detective would not focus on them

"Way to cool," Capone mumbled to himself.

"What was that?" Altamont asked.

"Nothing," Capone said as he smiled at Altamont. "I was saying I've got your back, that's all." He squeezed the great detective's hand.

Part Two

The phosphorus solution that Dr. Watson dripped for several miles led directly to an East London ships loading dock.

Dixie was waiting several hundred yards outside the entrance when Altamont, Yale and Capone pulled up in their hansom.

"They're just inside the dock. Dr. Watson is keeping an eye on them," Dixie said. "Mr. Johnson, did you have the crate you shipped from America placed in a metal container?"

"I did," confirmed Mr. Johnson. "I'm the only one with the key to the container."

"You were the only one with the key until it was sold this very evening," Altamont said. "I suspected that whoever trounced your room, when we first connected, was looking for something. It was the key to that metal bin. Mr. Yale, would you be so kind to work your way down the left flank of our South African friends, and Mr. Capone do the same to the right."

The two New York mobsters followed Altamont's instructions. The rest of the group joined Dr. Watson in the shadow of a very large shipping crate, hidden from the two thieves' vision. Kessler was inserting the key to the lock securing the metal bin.

"If they scratch my roadster, so help me God, there will be screaming, hollering and gnashing of teeth before I finish," Johnson said angrily.

"Quiet," Dr. Watson cautioned, still keeping his eyes peeled on the metal container.

The key fit the lock perfectly, and opened the metal door. The men took a lantern inside the metal bin, Kessler dug beneath the frame of Johnson's roadster where he had stashed the jewel, then emerged with the purple bag holding the diamond. He pulled the diamond out of the bag and lifted it in the air to watch the moonlight glisten from its smooth surface. They both were laughing heartily having recovered their precious jewel. Without warning to the men beside him, Altamont stepped into the open and started walking towards them.

"Stay hidden Watson," Altamont said. "Mr. Johnson and Mr. Dixie, with me."

When the South African laid eyes on the three men approaching, their eyes showed surprise, as if they saw a ghost. Johnson flashed a huge, hideous grin and the lamplight glinted off his gold tooth. "You're dead," Wilson said. "We saw those men hang you by the neck."

"Or so it seemed," Altamont said. "You were witnesses to an illusion designed by the great Harry Houdini."

The men reached for their guns but stopped short as Yale and Capone placed the barrels of their snubbed-nosed revolvers against the back of each man's neck. Kessler and Wilson never saw the two New York gangsters coming from behind.

"I'd drop those guns if I were you," Johnson said with an air of confidence. The South Africans complied and dropped their weapons. "I think you met the men with the guns to your head. Those boys are from New York and they run with a very nasty crowd. They would shoot you where you stand and think nothing of it later in the day."

"New York?" Kessler said with a raspy voice. "Why those bastards were part of a trap."

"A very good one at that," said Yale, who held his gun to Kessler's head. Then Yale brought the barrel of his gun down on the crown of Kessler's head, causing the big South African to stumble forward a few feet. "Our mother's were married. That's for the bastard comment."

"Told you those boys were mean," Johnson said with a snicker.

"Dr. Watson, be so kind as to retrieve the jewel?" Altamont said. "And Mr. Dixie, would you gather those guns from the ground?"

Dr. Watson appeared from the shadows and advanced towards the South Africans and took the jewel from Kessler's hands cautiously. Dixie scooped up their weapons. They returned to Altamont's side.

"Are you gentlemen sporting men?" Altamont asked innocently.

"Depends on the sport," Kessler said sourly.

"How would you like a chance to gain your freedom and get the jewel back?" Altamont continued.

"You'd do that?" Wilson inquired.

"You are both rather large men. And there is no secret South Africans hold no love in their heart for what you call in your country, *kaffers*, right?"

"True on both accounts," Kessler boasted. He had a hunch he knew where Altamont was going with the line of questioning.

"I will allow you to go free, and take the jewel with you, and we will say nothing of it, based on one condition," Altamont said.

"That being?" Kessler asked.

"You and your friend must engage in a bare-knuckles fist fight with both Mr. Johnson and Mr. Dixie until someone submits or are simply unable to continue," Altamont said. "If the both of you emerge the winners, then I will give you both freedom and jewels."

"Can you hold your end?" Johnson asked Dixie, looking him in the eyes. "I damn sure can hold mine. I haven't been in a street brawl for a while now. Don't forget to protect the solar plexus."

"I've wanted a piece of these boys since they jumped me at my flat days ago," Dixie said. "I want Kessler."

"Let's get started," Kessler said as he walked to the center of the dock, beckoning to Dixie. However, Wilson wasn't showing the same confidence. In fact, the color was leaving his cheeks, as he realized he had drawn a bout with the great Jack Johnson. Johnson pointed at Wilson, and blew him a kiss. Kessler and Dixie raised their fists. The hate for Dixie was apparent on Kessler's face. Dixie could not believe Kessler hated him so much; Kessler hated him for being a colored man. To him it made no sense. He didn't know the man, never did a thing to him, where was the anger coming from?

"WooooHoooo," Capone screamed at the top of his lungs. "I get to see the great Jack Johnson in a down and dirty street brawl. The boys will never believe this." He kept his gun trained on Wilson.

Dixie feigned a right punch that Kessler blocked but Dixie countered with a straight shot to his mouth with his left fist, causing Kessler to stumble back. It was something Johnson showed him when Johnson was giving him boxing tips. From there, the fight became brutal. Kessler and Dixie were landing punches against one another, but Dixie, thanks to Johnson's tips, was getting the upper hand. Blood was flowing from Kessler's mouth and Dixie's fists had opened a gash on his left eye. Kessler had landed an impressive left hook, however, and Dixie's right eye began swelling. Johnson estimated Dixie's fight with Kessler had gone a good five minutes. Neither man was trained for this type of fight, they both looked spent.

Johnson believed Kessler was fighting against his greatest fear; he did not want to be beaten by a colored man. Then the break Dixie needed occurred. Kessler threw a wild haymaker punch with his right fist. Dixie sidestepped, causing the exhausted Kessler to fall to the ground, on his back. The move was a classic side step Jack Johnson had shown him the night he and Johnson met. Dixie never let him get back up. Dixie pounced on Kessler and straddled his chest, reverting now to the old fashioned street brawler tactics he was known for. Dixie grabbed Kessler's shirt with his left hand, and began pounding Kessler's face with consecutive short, right hand punches. Kessler's face became a bloody mess, but he wasn't unconscious yet. Dixie continued, pounding, vaguely aware of what he was doing. He came to his senses when Altamont and Dr. Watson mercifully pulled him from atop Kessler. There was no doubt in his mind at that point, Kessler was unconscious.

Jack Johnson crooned as he handed Dixie a handkerchief to wipe the blood from his face and fist. Altamont and Dr. Watson dragged Kessler to Wilson's side and returned to their places. Wilson looked down at his unconscious friend. The look on his face was that of rage and fear.

"Damn," Yale said with a loud cackled laugh. "Did you see what Mr. Dixie did to your friend?"

Capone walked up behind Wilson and shoved him to the center of the dock.

"Your turn," Capone said to Wilson. "DINGGGGGGG!!!!!!!"

Conventional wisdom or at least it seemed for a reasonable man, would have been for Wilson to beg for mercy and ask to be taken immediately to the authorities. He chose unconventional wisdom. Instead, Wilson let out a loud kamikaze scream and ran furiously at Johnson throwing one of the most vicious punches known to man, thinking maybe he could end things with one punch. The confusion on his face was apparent, as he found nothing but air. Capone and Yale were doubling over with laughter. For the next few minutes the fight was much the same, Johnson slipping punch after punch, while he himself was yet to throw one. Poor Wilson. The energy he was expending with the wild array of disconnecting punches was taking a serious physical toll on his stamina. Yale and Capone marveled as the illusive Johnson ducked and dodged Wilson's hapless punches. Then suddenly the fight shifted. Johnson's right fist crashed violently against Wilson's nose. Everyone could hear the breaking of cartilage in Wilson's nostrils as he screamed. No sooner had that punch connected, Johnson countered with a solid left to Wilson's solar plexus, doubling Wilson over as the wind rushed from his lungs. Johnson closed the deal with a wicked closed fist to the back of Wilson's skull laying him out flat on his stomach, unconscious.

"Wilson must be certifiably crazy. Did you see the way he fights?" Johnson asked Altamont. Behind him Yale and Capone jumped and yelled in wonderment at the carnage they had just witnessed. "He fights like a woman. I'm hungry. Let's get back to Lady Hebron's house. I bet she's been cooking up a storm knowing we'll be coming back soon."

"Remind me never to get on your bad side, Mr. Johnson," Capone said, as he snickered while helping to lift Wilson's unconscious body.

The men loaded the unconscious South Africans into the two waiting hansoms and rode quietly back to Lady Hebron's house on the Westside of London. Altamont, who was in the hansom along with Johnson, the unconscious Wilson and Dixie, carefully examined the diamond.

As they stopped in front of Ms. Hebron's house, Johnson seemed distressed. "Oh no," he said, as he bolted out of the hansom and made his way to Lady Hebron's porch. Altamont gave chase behind him. There on the porch sat the two men The Fixer had left to protect Ms. Hebron's home. They were bound by ropes and their mouths gagged.

"A white man with an American accent wearing a cowboy hat and two of his Brit henchmen caught us by surprise. We never saw them coming," one of the colored men said. "They took Lady Hebron and left a note in my shirt pocket."

While Altamont released the men from their ropes, Johnson retrieved the note from the man's pocket and read aloud:

Mr. Johnson,

At 9 a.m. tomorrow morning, a hansom will arrive to pick you up. You get in and you will be brought to me. At that time, your lady friend will be released and sent home. Come alone and don't involve Scotland Yard. Tell your busybody cohorts not to interfere or she will die. You will not be returning to them.

Tex Cody – Bounty Hunter

"Lady Hebron has been too dear to us all," Johnson said to Altamont. "I'll comply with what this Cody fellow's wishes. Enough people have died because of me."

The guilt of the lives lost during the Independence Day evening, after his victory over Jim Jeffries was resurrected emotionally within Johnson. Lady Hebron's death would be too unbearable to count among them.

Chapter 11

The miniature Big Ben replica clock in Lady Hebron's living room struck midnight, but any sense of triumph that Johnson and the other five men felt, by bagging the two South Africans the day before, was overshadowed with concern for her safety as a new day was ushered in. Johnson sat quietly as Altamont made plans.

"Mr. Yale and Capone, perhaps you should book tickets on the *Mauretaina** for your journey back to New York at daylight. I'll need you to help an officer from Scotland Yard take our two South African jewel thieves and their stolen jewel to the New York authorities. The New York authorities will transport them back to Chicago, and investigate the origin of the jewel," Altamont said.

"No way. That is not going to happen," Yale said dryly. "We were sent to protect Mr. Johnson and he is in even more danger now. Plus, we've taken a liking to Lady Hebron. We want to help get her back. Right Alphonse?"

"Hell yeah," Capone said. "We'll keep these two South African punks tied in the back room. They're so beat up right now, if they gain consciousness, it will be a few hours before they can make heads-or-tails of where they are and what is going on. We'll have Lady Hebron by then."

"Well, Dr. Watson, I guess you can go home now," Johnson said. "You can't possibly think a half-breed woman would be worth your help, since you are a part of proper society."

"That is so unfair, Mr. Johnson. Lady Hebron is a fine woman and I will do everything in my power to help get her back," Dr. Watson replied.

"You called Ms. Hebron a half breed?" Capone asked the doctor. "I didn't think too much of you when we met, sir, but I think even less of you now."

"Oh, I think I'll survive the thought of a hired mobster, from New York, not holding me in high esteem," Dr. Watson retorted.

"So you think you're better than less fortunate people, do you, Dr. Watson?" Capone asked. "My family traveled to America as immigrants from Italy. They were poor, barely making it day-to-day. They worked hard to keep the family fed. People like you here in England, and people in America, look down their noses at us, seemingly content that immigrants remained in the slums of the Five Points*. If we ventured out, cops would harass us, arrest us, and beat us. They called themselves proper society too. I guess I can relate some to what Lady Hebron went through. Italian immigrants weren't considered worthy enough to be among proper society folks either. But had proper society really looked at Five Points, from a fair perspective, they would have found a lot of hard working people. They were people who were simply trying to make a better life for their families."

Johnson looked squarely at Dr. Watson for his response.

"I've read about this Five Points area in New York you speak of. You're right there are a lot of hard working people there. And if my memory serves me, hoodlums and gangsters like you, made these same hard working people pay protection money just to stay in business. If they didn't pay, they were brutalized. Right?" Dr. Watson asked Capone. "And am I to assume these same Italian immigrants embraced colored people with open arms? It seems to me you view things from hypocritical eyes."

Johnson saw Capone form a fist and move towards Dr. Watson, but Yale grabbed him. Johnson was glad Altamont interceded.

"I've had enough of this. All I've heard from present company are arguments about America's problems, and trying to correct America's problems here in Lady Hebron's living room is truly a waste of time. We're thousands of miles away," Altamont said. "There is a woman's life that hangs in the balance this very moment, right here in England, and all you can do is challenge one another's social morals. Let's put this aside until Lucy Hebron is safe. Then you may continue this useless debate. As I said earlier, these issues will still be discussed as we lay in our graves, well into the 21st century."

Johnson sat in a chair, shoulders hunched, and face with a saddened look. The house was like a morgue, cold and distant without Lady Hebron floating around bringing to the place lightness, a goodness. Tragedy seemed to strike any woman who came into his life. He wondered when it would end.

"You're right, Altamont. Lady Hebron is in danger because she was kind enough to allow me to hide away here until we got the South Africans. We never saw Tex Cody coming," Johnson said. "And I must confess, now that I think about it, I may have had a run-in with Tex Cody* years back when I was just breaking into the fight business. I beat him pretty badly back in Texas, in a bar brawl, and he vowed he would get me back for embarrassing him in front of his friends.

His friends feared him, they thought he was invincible, but after I beat him up, his friends lost respect for him. Looks like he's making good on that promise. There is a warrant for my arrest in America because of the Mann Act. He intends on getting his revenge and collecting the bounty for my return. That would be of great satisfaction for him."

"Not if we can help it," Dr. Watson said.

"Did Dr. Watson just show a sliver of humanity?" Capone asked sarcastically.

"I don't like bounty hunters and especially those arrogant enough to come across the pond from America, to England, and kidnap fine British citizens to satisfy his own gains," Dr. Watson said. "I admit I am extremely conservative, in many regards, but if Cody has an issue with Mr. Johnson, then no one as sweet and innocent as Lady Hebron should be used as a pawn to get back at him. I also must admit that the teamwork I saw when we executed Holmes' plan was impressive. I may have been a bit too judgmental about the men in this room."

"Well said, Watson, and I agree. However, this team has another mission ahead, and it is critical we devise a plan of attack. Since no one seems interested in leaving, until Lady Hebron is rescued, that means we remain on one accord. Whatever plan we come up with, it has to be in play and ready to execute at least by 9 a.m. this morning, when that hansom arrives to collect Mr. Johnson," Altamont said.

There was a knock at the door. Dixie walked to the front door and opened it. The two men who were there seemed astonished to see him.

"You're the last person I expected to see when calling on Mr. Sherlock Holmes," said Scotland Yard Inspector McKinnon*. "I'm sure you remember Inspector Youghal* from Scotland Yard, don't you, Mr. Dixie?"

"Ah yes, Scotland Yard's finest," responded Dixie. He said no more as he led them to the living room where Altamont and the rest of the men were. Johnson could only deduce that Dixie had run-ins with the two lawmen, and was probably still a suspect in the murder at Holborn Bar, which he understood from Altamont, was a case still under investigation.

"Mr. Holmes, we received your message. We have officers at Scotland Yard mobilized and at the ready," McKinnon said. "This is a terrible business, Mr. Holmes. Ms. Hebron is one of Britain's finest citizens."

"Mr. Holmes?" Yale asked, looking about the room at each man in the room. It was then he realized he was the only person there who did not know Altamont was indeed the great Sherlock Holmes. Now that he thought back, he remembered being perplexed why Lady Hebron had called him Mr. Holmes in earlier conversations. The smile on Capone's face confirmed his suspicions were correct.

"Alphonse, you knew and didn't tell me?" Yale asked, as if feeling deeply betrayed.

"In all fairness, my dear Mr. Yale, Mr. Capone didn't know until I made the mental blunder of using one of the sayings Dr. Watson has made famous in his chronicles of my adventures, while he rode with me earlier this evening," Altamont said.

Johnson knew how Yale felt. It still hadn't quite set in

with him that he was working alongside the great Sherlock Holmes.

"And now that you know, Mr. Yale, that information should only be said from your lips to God's ear," Johnson said. "Now Inspector McKinnon, does this Tex Cody have legal cause to apprehend me here on British soil?"

"When I received Mr. Holmes summons, I inquired at Scotland Yard and to this point the United States has not declared Mr. Johnson an international criminal. This fellow is obviously chasing Mr. Johnson at his own behest," Inspector Youghal said. "In most cases, an agent from foreign soil is required to register with Scotland Yard, at which time we assign an officer to assist him. We assign that officer to such foreign agents to make sure we keep up with his whereabouts, and that he stays within the framework of Great Britain's laws."

"So technically, your Mr. Cody is moving as an independent agent outside the jurisdiction of Scotland Yard's permission," Inspector McKinnon said.

"No surprise there," Johnson said. Altamont chimed in.

"I have a friend in America who is fairly well placed in the American law enforcement community," Altamont said. "Inspector McKinnon, do you think I can use your international telephone line to contact the man? It's almost midnight here. That means it is late afternoon in the United States. I'm sure he'll put in a couple of hours to help us."

"Well let us make haste to Scotland Yard, Mr. Holmes," Inspector McKinnon said.

"Inspector Youghal, can you get to the lower East End and talk with some of your constables on the street? Surely a man of such low caliber would feel more comfortable moving in that environment," Altamont said. "Mr. Dixie, take Mr. Capone and Yale to local pubs. Use Mr. Capone's and Mr. Yale's New York style of persuasion if need be, but get someone to talk. Someone has to have seen this Tex Cody. He won't be at the pubs this hour, because if I'm correct, he will not let Lady Hebron out of his sight. Dr. Watson, remain here with the South Africans until we return."

"South Africans?" Inspector Youghal asked.

"Go Inspector Youghal," Inspector McKinnon urged. "I'm just as curious as you are, but time is fleeting, and I'm sure Mr. Holmes will explain the way. One thing I've learned, Mr. Holmes methodology may be unpredictable, but in such matters he can be trusted."

Part Two

Johnson traveled to Scotland Yard with Altamont and marvelled. His detective antennas stretched into America. He listened intently to Holmes' conversation with New York City Police Department (NYPD) detective, Tony Soprano.

"Mr. Sherlock Holmes, what a pleasure to hear from you. It was a pleasure meeting you last summer," said Detective Soprano. "It is almost divine intervention that you should call this very day. My bureau here in New York got wind that two of the Mafia's up and coming mobsters are in England. Apparently sent to execute one of your British subjects."

"Would you be referring to Frankie Yale and Alphonse Capone?"

"Well I'll be. Yeah, how did you know their names?" Soprano asked.

"They have been invaluable agents for me in solving a jewel heist that took place in Chicago," Altamont said. "They were sent to protect, not kill. In fact, they will be sailing back to New York on the *Mauretaina* in a few days. They will help a Scotland official escort two South African jewel thieves and a stolen jewel back to your country tomorrow. I'll be sure to send a note detailing the whole affair. However, I would appreciate it if you make mention that you, Detective Soprano and the NYPD, worked in unison with Scotland Yard in the whole affair. I can ill afford for the public to know I've been in partnership with mobsters."

"That is mighty kind of you Mr. Holmes. But do you realize how dangerous Yale and Capone are?" Detective Soprano asked.

"Dangerous? They have been quite instrumental, in their own way of course, in helping me solve the Chicago jewel heist. Now they are assisting me in recovering a kidnapped woman. A woman, I might add, who is as dear to them, as she is to me," Altamont said.

"Yale? Capone? On the side of the law?" Detective Soprano asked curiously. "Don't send the scoundrels back, if that's the case. Sounds like the British atmosphere has some real power floating in the air to rehabilitate criminal elements."

"You must promise me another thing," Altamont said. "When Mr. Capone and Mr. Yale return to New York, you cannot breathe a word of their helping me, or Scotland Yard, for their sake. Their underworld connections would not take too kindly to such a thing. My God, it would sully their criminal reputations; their street credibility would be ruined." In the background, silently, Inspector McKinnon was doubled over in laughter, face reddening, upon hearing Holmes' oxymoron. During the hansom ride to Scotland Yard, Altamont had told him of the men's' dubious association with organized crime.

"Huh?" Detective Soprano exclaimed.

"Never mind, the report will explain everything," Altamont continued. "However, Detective Soprano, I need you to gather as much information about a gentleman named Tex Cody."

"You have Tex Cody there in London with you, too?" Soprano asked, with even more interest. "You have a regular den of iniquity surrounding you, Mr. Holmes, with Yale and Capone there. And now you say you have Cody there in England with you? We just received a national bulletin for

Cody's arrest. Seems that low life, Mr. Cody, has taken liberty with an underage young lady in the state of Texas."

"Are we talking statutory rape?" Altamont inquired.

"Absolutely. She is 15-years-old and is now pregnant. The worst part, if there is a worst part in this situation, is she is the daughter of a powerful legislator in the Lone Star state. He wants Tex Cody's butt in the worst way," Detective Soprano concluded.

"Outstanding," Altamont said with glee.

"Excuse me?" Detective Soprano bellowed.

"Oh, no, don't get me wrong Detective Soprano. I'm just as disgusted that Cody took advantage of an underage girl. But I believe it outstanding we may be able to deliver him to you in New York," Altamont said. "We may be able to send him back with the South African jewel thieves. That would be a major coup for you. I have an Inspector McKinnon here with me at Scotland Yard. He will probably assign an Inspector Youghal to accompany the three criminals if all goes well. I'll be in touch."

Johnson shook his head in amazement. Tex Cody, the hunter, in one phone call, had become the hunted.

"We must hurry to Lady Hebron's place," Altamont said, with urgency in his voice. "I only hope the other will have a good report."

Part Three

    Johnson, Altamont and Inspector McKinnon entered Lucy Hebron's living room where everyone was waiting. There was a Scotland Yard constable and a woman seated along with them.

    Johnson nodded his head with approval as Inspector Youghal gave his report first. "Mr. Holmes, this is Constable Gregg." Gregg stood to shake Altamont's hand. "He was patrolling his ward tonight and saw three men pulling a woman out of a hansom."

    "What an honor to meet you Mr. Holmes," Constable Gregg said, shaking Holmes' hand enthusiastically. Then he shared his information. "One of the gentlemen was a colored fellow, and it was he who held the unconscious colored woman in his arms, as they took her into the building. I asked him what was wrong with her. He said they were at a local bar and she had too much to drink. He said the other gentlemen, who were white, were helping him get her to the flat. He said she was his wife. One of the white gentlemen was American that I'm sure of. No chap in London wears cowboy boots and cowboy Stetson."

    "Ahhh, that's our man. And obviously they chloroformed Lady Hebron to render her unconscious," Altamont said. "Do remember the flat in which they entered?"

    "Clear as a bell," Constable Gregg said.

    Then Altamont turned his attention to the strange woman who was seated in the living room.

    "Excellent," Altamont said. "And who is this young lady?"

"I'm Lucille, Mr. Holmes," said the middle-aged woman, as she stood to shake his hand. Altamont kept a straight face as the smell of alcohol from her breath invaded his nostrils.

"We met Lucille at the second pub we went to," Mr. Yale said. "It seems she spent a few hours in our cowboy's company, at his flat."

"Obviously not playing gin rummy," Dr. Watson said sourly.

"No, we weren't, you fat toad," Lucille retorted.

"I knew I liked this woman," Capone interjected, as he emitted a snicker.

"Let us stay focused on the business at hand," Altamont said. "Excuse my friends, Ms. Lucille."

"Already have you sweet man," Lucille said as she stroked Altamont's arm seductively.

"Geez," Dr. Watson said, after witnessing Lucille's amorous advance towards Altamont.

"And that cheap American was no gentleman," Lucille continued. "I think I gave him the best hours of his life and then he threw me out without paying me. He told me he'd kill me if I came back for money."

Altamont reached into his pocket, and handed money to Lucille.

"This should more than cover your compensation for that night. There is additional money if you can get him to open his door to the flat," Altamont bargained.

"And I don't get to spend time with you?" Lucille asked.

There was a giggle expelled throughout the room. Altamont's face reddened.

"No, Ms. Lucille, I'm afraid not. I'll pay handsomely for you to just get him to open his door," Altamont clarified.

"Okay. But you'll never know what you're missing out on," Lucille assured him. She placed the palm of her hand firmly on Altamont's butt cheeks and gave them a loving squeeze.

Altamont leaped forward, surprised at Lucille's love advance. "Ms. Lucille, how dare you," Altamont said.

By now, the giggles in the living room had erupted into a loud roar of laughter.

Chapter 12

Johnson, Constable Gregg, Inspector McKinnon, Inspector Youghal and Lucille were in the lead hansom as they pulled within a block of Tex Cody's flat. Altamont, Dr. Watson, Capone, Yale and Dixie all squeezed into the hansom that followed.

Johnson led the contingent quietly to within twenty-five yards of Cody's flat. It was 6 a.m.

"There," Constable Gregg pointed to the front flat on the right side of an apartment building. "They turned the light on when they entered. It is still lit. I'm sure that is the flat."

"Yep, that's the flat where that low life lives," Lucille confirmed.

Johnson looked at Altamont. "I'm going in, don't even think I won't. But we have too many people to enter at one time. It looks like a narrow entrance to the flat."

Altamont nodded. "Lucille, you'll go to the door, knock, get Cody to answer, and once he does, then Constable Gregg you pull her back and take her outside. Mr. Johnson, as soon as you see a crack in the door, I want you to kick it in. When the door is kicked open, Mr. Yale and Mr. Capone, I want the two of you to enter the room first to secure it."

Inspector Youghal objected. "Wait a minute, Mr. Holmes. For the sake of our ongoing relationship, I have remained silent about Mr. Yale and Mr. Capone even being here on British soil. They are criminals by your own admission for Christ's sake. I really should have them locked up and sent back to America this very moment. You have trained law enforcers in Inspector McKinnon and me. If anyone is going through that door first it will be us."

"Inspector Youghal, I understand your concern. I am asking you to indulge me, call it a calculated deduction if you will. You trusted my instinct in past cases. Will you trust them once more?" Altamont said.

Inspector Youghal looked at the two mobsters and then Altamont. "Okay, but you better be right about this one, Mr. Holmes."

"Outstanding, Inspector Youghal," Altamont said. "Shall we?"

Once inside the apartment entrance, Lucille knocked gingerly at the door. No answer. Lucille knocked again. The cock of a gun trigger could be heard clearly on the other side of the door.

"Who is it?" Cody asked.

"Its Lucille, baby," Lucille cooed in a seductive voice.

"I told you I'd kill you if you came back for money," Cody said sternly.

"No baby, I don't want money. I'm burning hot thinking of the other night. I need a repeat performance you cowboy stud," Lucille said.

Johnson didn't know what it was about the comforts of a woman, that makes even the strongest man weak, but if there was a sucker for such a weakness, it had to be Tex Cody. He must have had a very high opinion of his abilities in bed, because he bought Lucille's story hook-line-and-sinker.

"Now you're talking," Cody said. Johnson heard him close the trigger of his gun. As Cody opened the door ever so slightly, Johnson saw a smile on his face. The smile disappeared quickly as Constable Gregg grabbed Lucille and pulled her back from the door. Johnson kicked the door with all his might flush into Cody's face. Cody tumbled backwards into the flat. Johnson moved out of the way. Capone and Yale entered the flat, snubbed-nose revolvers at the ready.

The white Brit who was working with Cody reached for his gun as he stood up. Yale fired a shot that pierced through the man's upper right arm. The man howled in pain, while falling to the floor and clutching his arm. When Cody's colored partner reached for his pistol, he made eye contact with Capone. Capone didn't speak, but his eyes dared the man to lift his weapon, on Capone's face shown a murderous sneer. Capone kicked Cody's pistol towards the door where Inspector McKinnon picked it up as he entered.

Johnson moved in at that point and landed a punch flush to Cody's right jaw, knocking Cody back to the floor. Johnson straddled Cody's chest, and delivered left then right combination punches, incapacitating the stunned Cody. Constable Gregg went directly to the now conscious Lucy Hebron, cut loose her bindings, and escorted her out of the room to safety.

"Looking for me Cody? Kidnapping innocent women to lure me here? I'm here," Johnson said, delivering yet another solid right hand to the already bloody face of Tex Cody.

Altamont entered the room once the villains were neutralized.

"Please Dr. Watson, would you be so kind as to tend to that gentleman's wound?" Altamont said, as he pointed to Cody's white henchman squirming in pain, from the bullet lodged in his arm. "Inspectors McKinnon and Youghal, what did you witness in regards to the gentleman who Mr. Yale shot in the arm?"

"Clear case of self-defense as far as I'm concerned," Inspector McKinnon said. "And you Inspector Youghal?"

"Oh, definitely, self-defense. I'd go as far as to say the gentleman who was shot may have been about to shoot Mr. Capone. Plenty of witnesses to verify it," Inspector Youghal said.

At that point, Lucille rushed into the room, kicking Cody directly in his crotch.

"Ohhhhhhhh, ouch!" Capone said with a chuckle. Inspector McKinnon grabbed Lucille and escorted her out the flat. Cody rolled into a fetal position, cradling his family jewels.

"Didn't want to pay me you low life. Now you'll really pay," Lucille screamed on the way out the door.

"Is it me?" Altamont asked Cody. "Or do you get the feeling some people in this room aren't happy to see you? Please Mr. Johnson; help Mr. Cody to a chair."

At that point, Altamont pulled a chair directly in front of Cody. He pulled out his pipe, packed it with tobacco, and puffed contently, until it appeared Tex Cody was able to talk.

"It has been a long night and even more stressful morning, Mr. Cody," Altamont said coolly. "So far you're looking at attempted murder, kidnapping, pulling a weapon on British civil servants and resisting arrest. Am I on target, Inspector McKinnon?"

"Totally accurate," Inspector McKinnon said.

"Now, Mr. Cody, I advise you forget bounty pay. You see, you are being taken back to America, a wanted felon from what I understand," Altamont said.

"What is he wanted for?" Yale asked.

"It appears Mr. Cody is a father. The mother is 15-years-old and pregnant. Her father, a prominent politician in Texas, put out a nationwide alert in America for the capture of Mr. Cody. Mr. Capone, Mr. Yale, do you have any young ladies, that age, in your family?" Altamont asked.

"Oh yeah," Yale said. "Alphonse, and I, both."

"Are you willing to write a confession Mr. Cody? Admitting to statutory rape with the underage child in Texas? Then after that, write a confession about kidnapping Lady Hebron?" Altamont asked Cody, looking him straight into his eyes.

"Go spit, you stupid Brit," Cody said vehemently. Then something seemed to dawn on him. "You called that guy Yale. Is that Frankie Yale, from the New York crime family?"

"One in the same," Yale answered.

Altamont had found Cody's weakness. He not only knew Frankie Yale but he feared him. Cody feared his mob reputation.

"Well, this stupid Brit is going to leave and he's going to take that wounded friend of yours. The Scotland Yard inspectors who probably could save you, they are leaving too," Altamont said dryly. "I'll leave you, Mr. Cody, with Mr. Yale and his associate Mr. Capone. They seem to have an aversion to men who prey on underage girls. They have young girls in their family that age. They may want to readjust your attitude in that regard."

"What about me?" Cody's colored associate asked.

"If you're willing to write a confession about your role in helping Mr. Cody kidnap Lady Hebron, you'll be leaving with us. If not, I'll leave you to talk the matter over with Mr. Jack Johnson, who by the way is a very close friend of Lady Hebron," Altamont said. He stood and walked to the door. Dr. Watson helped the wounded accomplice and they all disappeared through the door, leaving Cody and his colored accomplice in the room with Johnson, Yale and Capone.

Johnson gave the colored accomplice an evil smile as he began removing his jacket. Before the door could shut, the colored accomplice screamed at the top of his lungs, as he stared into Johnson's menacing eyes.

"I'll sign, I'll sign," the colored accomplice screamed. "I'll be damn if you're leaving me in here alone with Jack Johnson."

Despite themselves, Yale and Capone snickered to a point their bodies shook. The aim of their snub-nosed revolvers never left Cody however.

Altamont stuck his head back through the door.

"Bring him along, Mr. Johnson," Altamont said.

Johnson shoved the colored accomplice towards the door. "I'll stay. I want to enjoy watching Cody take this Mafia style beating."

"As you wish," Altamont said. "I'll leave Constable Gregg outside the door so no one will disturb the four of you. Good day to you Mr. Cody."

Altamont closed the door. Yale and Capone began pulling their jackets off. Capone pulled a set of brass knuckles from his jacket pocket, carefully placing them on his right fist.

Cody tried a desperate bolt from his chair to the door, but Yale smashed his snub-nosed revolver against his skull, dropping Cody to his knees.

"I'm offended Mr. Cody," Capone said as he walked towards Cody. "You don't seem to cherish our company. I guess you seem to think the company of a vulnerable 15-year-old girl is more preferable? What did you do, Mr. Cody, since you're uglier than sin? Did you rape her? Force her to lay with you?"

At that moment, Cody squealed from the force of Capone's brass knuckles crashing on his face. This was how Capone and Yale handled things in New York for the mob. The men they dealt with were killers and pimps. The men they dealt with feared only one thing, someone more vicious than they were.

"Stand him up Mr. Yale," Capone said coolly. As Yale held Cody upright, Capone delivered a cruel blow to Cody's ribcage and a snap could be heard within the room. As Cody fell he hadn't noticed Yale had slipped on brass knuckles as well.

"This is how we deal with child molesters in New York," Yale said, as he dealt another crushing, brass knuckles aided punch, to Cody jaw. Blood spurted from Cody's mouth and he spat out several teeth.

Johnson watched as he stood in front of the door. He wondered if Yale and Capone were aware of Diamond Jim Colosimo's prostitution business, in Chicago. That this enterprise was staffed by scores of kidnapped, under aged girls. He wondered if they knew that the nature of Colosimo's business meant once those girls were brought in, they were beaten and raped into submission, forced to do the will of their pimps. Johnson wondered how Capone and Yale* viewed that travesty? This is what Johnson hated about the criminal world. They all had willingness, as criminals, to overlook obvious wrongs, simply because they shared the Mafioso oath. Johnson knew that Dixie loved his own cousin as a son, and condemned The Rat for betraying his cousin. But Johnson knew that Dixie knew what his cousin did. Dixie knew his cousin was stealing and buying weaponry, and selling them on the black market to various dangerous and nefarious criminal elements. Some of those weapons had been used against England probably.

Capone drove his brass knuckles into Cody's head, just behind the right ear and Cody fell to the floor. The door opened, Altamont entered to intervene. Johnson knew if this kept up, Yale and Capone would kill Cody. Johnson didn't care. He wanted Cody dead. Johnson knew Altamont had allowed this carnage to take place, but he also knew Altamont, deep within, did not approve of these tactics. But these were violent times and such matters had to be dealt with just as violently.

"Dr. Watson is a compassionate man, Mr. Cody," Altamont said as he motioned for the two New York mobsters to refrain. "He thought I should come back and give you one last chance to consent to writing a confession. He heard your ribcage crack on the other side of the door. He said he thought he heard your jaw shatter as well. What do you say, Mr. Cody? Ready to cooperate?"

"Yes," Cody said faintly, while suffering pain, coursing throughout his body.

"Excuse me," Altamont said. "Couldn't hear you?"

"Yes, Yes, I'll write a confession," Cody said louder.

The New York mobsters were disappointed. They were just getting started with what they did best as a vocation.

"All offenses, Mr. Cody?" Altamont asked. "You will give written confession to kidnapping Lady Hebron, raping the young girl and attempted murder by shooting at Mr. Johnson?"

"Yes, all offenses," Cody said. The pain he felt was excruciating. He knew his life would have been extinguished if he were left alone in that room with Capone and Yale any longer. He knew their reputation well, since he had dealings in the New York underworld. The two were killers.

"Would you be so kind, gentlemen, as to help me escort this man to Scotland Yard?" Altamont said to Yale and Capone.

The New York mobsters lifted Cody and draped his arms on their shoulders. Cody howled from pain.

"Oh shut up," Capone told him as they exited the flat. "You should be singing with joy, because had it not been for Altamont, we surely would have killed you back there, you dirt bag."

Cody merely grunted. He knew Capone meant what he said.

A hansom was commissioned to take Lucille home while two more took the entire team back to Scotland Yard.

Johnson joined Dr. Watson and Altamont as they sat on a lobby bench inside the Scotland Yard headquarters. He was silent, content to listen to Dr. Watson.

"Holmes, this was one of the most violent cases we've ever been involved with. Without doubt, we were in league with some of the seediest characters ever," Dr. Watson said.

"My dear Dr. Watson, any case we've had has involved

the criminal element, so everyone falls under that "seedy" classification if you ask me," Holmes said.

As for the level of violence, Johnson listened, as Holmes shared his own perspective.

"I tend also to disagree with you, regarding the violence level," Holmes said, puffing contently on his pipe. "The men we engaged the last few days are child's play when compared to the diabolical plots of Professor Moriaty. How we reacted in Professor Moriarty's cases were merely what was needed to be done. Had that predicated more violence, I'm sure we would have complied. No, Dr. Watson, you must understand that the cast of characters, who graced the stages of this adventure. Each person in this tale are as anomalous as Mr. Johnson, they simply should not exist, per today's standards. The men whom we formed a partnership with the past few days are men who live their lives in worlds enveloped by violence. They simply did what they always do in the world in which they evolve. They simply reacted with acts of superior violence. Did you see the fight between Mr. Johnson and Wilson? Wilson never landed a punch. Mr. Johnson simply let Wilson expend his violent rage and then finished him off just as he has done countless times in the ring. And what about Mr. Yale and Mr. Capone, when we invaded Tex Cody's flat? Had we sent Inspectors McKinnon and Youghal in first, they would have hesitated when guns were drawn. Not our New York mobsters. In their world it is pull the trigger first or be shot, kill first or be killed.* They did what came natural. We simply witnessed self-preservation in its most elementary of forms."

"That Capone scares me," Dr. Watson admitted.

"And to think he has that affect on you, Dr. Watson, and then remember, Mr. Capone is only a teenager," Johnson said. "That Capone kid is headed for greatness*, that much I'm sure of. Whether it will be on the right side of the law is the million dollar question."

Inspectors McKinnon and Youghal walked out to the lobby along with Capone and Yale. The two South Africans and Tex Cody accompanied them, weighted down with irons on both their wrist and ankles. Every step Cody took seemed painful.

"We're escorting the prisoners, Mr. Capone and Mr. Yale to the *Mauretaina*," Inspector McKinnon said. "On behalf of Scotland Yard, Mr. Holmes, we owe you and Dr. Watson our deepest gratitude, as always. Mr. Dixie, I thought I'd never hear myself say this, but Scotland Yard owes you a debt of gratitude as well. Mr. Holmes shared with me what you have done the past few days. This is a great opportunity for you Mr. Dixie; from here you have a chance to stay on the right side of the law. Please take the opportunity. As an additional token of thanks, our inspectors have been instructed to "bury" the current case file we're investigating that involves you. Keep your nose clean, and it will stayed buried."

Dixie smiled. The words were like manna from heaven.

"Mr. Johnson, I'm sorry you had to go through all of this on Her Majesty's soil. Here is my card," Inspector McKinnon said, handing Johnson his business card. "Call on me if you have anymore trouble."

"Mr. Capone and Mr. Yale, I believe this will conclude our business," Mr. Johnson said as he handed them each an envelope full of American money. "I had doubts you could help me when I saw how young you were, but gentleman, I'll be the first to admit I was wrong. My goodness, you will both go far* in what you guys call 'this thing of ours.' Thank you again."

Capone and Yale both shook Johnson's hand and thanked him sincerely. They also shook Altamont's hand vigorously.

"Your identity Altamont is safe with us, from our lips to God's ear," Yale said, while he winked at Johnson.

Yale shook Dr. Watson's hand and followed the inspectors towards the door. Johnson smiled as Capone shook Dr. Watson's hand, but fired one last verbal barb. In reality, he had grown to like the old cuss.

"If you're ever in New York, Dr. Watson, don't look me up. I might shoot you," Mr. Capone said with a giggle.

"And Mr. Capone, if you're ever back in England and find yourself in a hospital bed, be sure you know whose behind the surgeon's mask administering your medication," Dr Watson said in return, also laughing.

Capone placed a friendly hand on Dr. Watson's shoulder, then left.

Johnson walked with Dixie through the door leading out of Scotland Yard. Altamont and Dr. Watson walked with them. Johnson enjoyed the cool breeze that brushed past his face. London's morning fog rendered the landscape a hazy backdrop of gray.

"Mr. Johnson, my anomalous friend, you're free to return to your flat," Altamont said. "What will you do from here?"

"I'm thinking about going to France* and see if I can't

strike a deal with fight promoters here in London. Maybe the Frenchmen will set up a fight for me. The French seem to embrace colored celebrities from America. I might even start a world war*," Johnson said, with a laugh. "I will have to go back to America to serve that ridiculous prison sentence* eventually. I'll see Europe a bit before I do."

Johnson turned to Dixie and to Dixie's surprise, Johnson embraced him with a hug.

"My dear friend, Mr. Steve Dixie, you remained at my side from the time that bullet landed in the dirt just inches from me to this very moment. I shall never forget you my dear friend," Johnson said.

Johnson remembered that Dixie had paid The Fixer's men out of his own pocket to protect Johnson. Johnson handed him an envelope full of cash.

"If you refuse to take this we'll have to put on boxing gloves, because you'll have to knock me out and place the money on my unconscious body to give it back," Johnson said.

"I'd better accept it then, because men far more skilled with boxing gloves have not been able to do what you require of me," Dixie said.

Dixie then turned to Holmes and Dr. Watson.

"Mr. Holmes, I mean Altamont, and Dr. Watson; I leave you a changed man. Don't let them talk about me too bad, unless you remind them of the good I've done the past few days," Dixie said to them both as he shook their hands. Dixie turned and walked away quickly. He did not want them to see his tears. Tough guys don't cry he reminded himself, as he moved slowly into the fog.

"Come to my flat one day," Johnson told Dixie. "I'll take you to the pub and fry some of my American chicken for you again."

However, a frantic voice was audible into London's evening fog. It was the young sentry who had patted Dixie down at his cousin's warehouse. Johnson knew Dixie would never forget the words the young sentry screamed.

"Mr. Dixie, your cousin has been shot, and is at the hospital in East London," the lad told him as he approached. "The doctors say his condition is grave."

Dixie expelled a breath full of anger.

Chapter 13

Johnson watched as the young sentry, who had shown so much allegiance to The Fixer, speak franticly.

"You must come to the hospital immediately," the young sentry said. "He is in a bad way. He has a head injury from falling when he took a gunshot to his chest."

"Calm down son," Johnson said. "When did this shooting occur?"

"The inspectors from Scotland Yard think early this morning, close to 1 a.m.," the young sentry said, trying hard to catch his breath.

While Dixie was upset with the abrupt news, he tried to calm the young sentry.

"Now take it easy son. Where is my cousin?" Dixie asked.

"The hospital on the East End. I'll take you to him," the sentry said.

"And do you know who is behind this?" Johnson asked.

"The Rat, it had to be. After I delivered the message you sent your cousin, your cousin told me he suspected The Rat was working against him with a rival arms dealer," The sentry replied.

Inspector McKinnon made his way to Johnson and Dixie, a look of concern and caution upon his face.

"Mr. Dixie I know you want to see your cousin but I insist you come by to see me tomorrow. We have some questions about what shenanigans your cousin might have been involved in. One of Scotland Yard's street sources alerted Scotland Yard recently about some disturbing business he suspected your cousin was involved in. Whatever it was, it caused someone to try and murder him," Inspector McKinnon said.

"Am I a suspect now, after you made that speech about burying my file?" Dixie asked.

"No, no you are not a suspect, Mr. Dixie. You are, however, his nearest kin, that we at Scotland Yard know. Perhaps you can shed some light that may give us a lead on his assailant," Inspector McKinnon said. "Can I count on your cooperation? Will you come to my office in the morning?"

Johnson realized this was indeed a strange twist for Dixie. In the past when Inspector McKinnon wanted to question Dixie, the inspector would send constables to retrieve him. But now the inspector was showing Dixie some respect, asking for his presence. Johnson and Dixie knew this was a huge a step in the right direction for Dixie in gaining the inspector's trust.

"I'll be there Inspector McKinnon. Say, around 11 a.m.?" Dixie asked.

"That will be fine," Inspector McKinnon agreed. "Now go see that cousin in the hospital."

Inspector McKinnon watched Johnson, Dixie and the young sentry scamper into the night to hail a hansom. The inspector knew The Fixer was knee deep in black market weapons sales, to factions not friendly to the Royal Crown. Deep in his gut, Inspector McKinnon knew Dixie was not involved. Dixie was a simple street level thug with plenty of street credibility. Bashing heads was his mantra. And there was an unsolved murder that pointed directly to The Fixer but all the evidence was not there. All Scotland Yard had was a written accusation by one of The Fixer's close associates. An associate with a dubious background.

The hospital was befitting of the East End of London. The building was antiquated in structure, and had a dank smell in the hallways when one entered. It was a skeleton crew of third shift staff that manned the hospital, but the guard at the door remembered Dixie's cousin when he was admitted. He directed the three men to The Fixer's area. The Fixer's bed was located in an open space where several beds were located. Dixie came to an abrupt halt by the cousin's bedside, more surprised than anything else. There stood Dr. Watson at his cousin's bedside accompanied by a young nurse. Dr. Watson was giving her instructions.

"Nurse we'll need to keep this area of his chest clean since it is a pretty serious gunshot wound. And did you find the doctor who attended him when he first arrived?" Dr. Watson asked her. "And make a note on his chart instructing every nurse that attends him, I want the wound redressed every four hours. We need to keep that wound as clean and antiseptic as possible, despite the God forsaken conditions in this wretched infirmary."

Dr. Watson looked up. His eyes met Dixie's. Dixie's face showed absolute amazement mixed with gratitude. In fact, his eyes began to well with tears.

"For goodness sake man don't get all misty eyed," Dr. Watson, said. "We'll get this young man through this, and then I'm going to sit him down and have a long talk about the company he keeps. He's unconscious now Mr. Dixie, and has been since his arrival. But he's a tough one for sure. I've seen men die of such wounds before, if they even made it to the hospital. Chin up old boy."

Johnson knew the tears Dr. Watson saw in Dixie's eyes weren't those solely of concern for his cousin. Dixie, Johnson realized, was overwhelmed by Dr. Watson's presence at his cousin's bedside.

"Mr. Dixie, when Holmes and I heard about your cousin's calamity, I came here immediately. I know the care a patient gets at this East End hospital is below standards compared to hospitals in some of London's more prestigious facilities," Dr. Watson said. "While I may not be considered an elite doctor, I am highly competent, and for a friend such as you, I'll use my skills to the utmost to keep this young man alive. Holmes went to the warehouse where your cousin headquarters, you'll find him there. You can help your cousin more at the warehouse. I'll make sure your cousin is cared for properly in the mean time."

Johnson's heart was warmed. He knew Dr. Watson's juxtaposition overwhelmed Dixie. The best Dixie could do was walk to the doctor and shake his hand. Both he and Dr. Watson knew no words need be exchanged. Johnson brought Dixie back in focus.

"Let's go to the warehouse," Johnson said. Johnson grabbed Dixie's arm and the men exited the hospital. The sentry flagged down a hansom and they rode to the warehouse. As Johnson entered the warehouse, he saw Altamont peering through his magnifying glass, at documents spread on a table before him. Constables from Scotland Yard were going through a second round of interrogations with The Fixer's men. Even Lady Hebron had come to the warehouse looking for them after hearing the news. She approached Johnson and Dixie with a package of food still warm in her hands.

"This is for the two of you. I brought enough for everyone, however," Lady Hebron said. She glanced around the busy crime scene and confided in Johnson. "Never been this close to the action. I must admit, to watch how astutely Mr. Holmes goes about his work, is amazing. He is so focused."

"How did you hear about his shooting?" Johnson asked.

"They sent a constable to my home. They thought maybe everyone was still at my place. I insisted he bring me back with him. That was, however, after I cooked you all a meal."

"Lady Hebron you should be at home resting," Johnson said. "You were chloroformed into unconsciousness, and held captive for God's sake. What are you doing here?"

"I'm standing by my friends, just like they were there for me, in my time of need," Lady Hebron said. She grabbed Dixie by the arm and guiding him to a chair. "Now eat while it's still warm. Mr. Johnson, the chair beside Mr. Dixie, please be seated there."

The men were hungry and delighted to open their packages to find heavily layered beef sandwiches. They consumed the sandwiches quickly, which indicated they were hungrier than they thought. It had been a while since Johnson or Dixie had eaten. They hadn't had time to eat with such a busy day. As Johnson inserted the last bite into his mouth, Johnson's gold tooth glistened in the warehouse light as he smiled, satisfied with his meal. Johnson spotted a constable walking towards Altamont with a small man with him. He looked like a street urchin, a man who lived in the streets. The constable introduced him as George, just as Johnson and Dixie joined Altamont's side. Altamont had sent the constable to scour the streets for witnesses who could shed light on The Fixer's shooting.

"This gentleman said he was knocked to the ground by a white man who was running from the warehouse," the constable said.

"The scoundrel never even stopped to help me up or see if I was all right," George said. "He and another colored fellow were running for their lives it seems. That white scoundrel dropped this in his rush to get away." George handed Altamont a note.

"Meet me at the warehouse. Your brother is there. The documents are there as well," Altamont said as he read the note aloud. The sentry and Lady Hebron had joined Altamont, Dixie and Johnson.

"Mr. Dixie is your mother still living?" Altamont asked, turning to Dixie.

"Yes, but she is very old, but her mind is still sharp as a tack," Dixie answered. "Surely she doesn't have anything to do with this business."

"Directly, no, but I have a hunch. Did she have a sister?" Altamont said.

"Yes," Dixie replied. "The Fixer's mother."

"Take me to her, Mr. Dixie. Mr. Johnson, accompany us if you will," Altamont said. "If my premonitions are correct, she may have a clue to what I suspect will turn out to be a rather sordid affair."

Johnson had his reservations about Altamont's

premonition, but he was, in reality, the great Sherlock Holmes, so he agreed. Altamont gave the sentry money to take Lady Hebron home.

The hansom ride was a short one, to another run down section of the East End. Dixie's mother lived in a squalor row of apartments. Dixie knocked on the door and upon answering the door, Dixie's mother's eyes flashed with excitement at seeing her son. Her expression turned to disappointment when she saw Altamont and Johnson.

"Boy, what kind of trouble you in now?" Mrs. Dixie asked. "Every time I see you with a white man, you're in some kind of trouble, usually with the law."

"My name is Altamont," Altamont said extending his right hand to shake that of Mrs. Dixie. "I'm pleased to tell you, that on this occasion at least, your son is working on the side of the law. It was I who asked him to bring me here. May I speak with you?"

Mrs. Dixie gave Altamont a suspicious look. "And who are you?" Mrs. Dixie asked Johnson.

"Jack Johnson, from America," Johnson replied.

"Come on in. Tea?" she asked. "Or perhaps I can fix you both something to eat?"

"No thank you but we appreciate the offer. Please have a seat. I need you to be totally honest with me regarding the question I'm about to pose to you," Altamont said. "Mr. Dixie said you have a sister, am I correct?"

"Yes, but Hattie passed on to be with the Lord," Mrs. Dixie said.

"Did she have sons?" Altamont asked.

"Just one son, and he like his cousin, decided to do the devil's work," Mrs. Dixie said, a tone of disappointment apparent in her voice. Altamont knew she was referring to The Fixer. "What kind of trouble that boy done got himself into now?"

"He has been shot, Momma," Dixie informed her. His mother's head lowered as she shook her head.

"That's not absolutely true is it? That she had just one son?" Altamont pressed on.

Mrs. Dixie looked into Altamont eyes and knew he suspected something.

"What is this all about?" Mrs. Dixie asked Altamont, point blank.

"England's national security, if my suspicions serve me correctly," Altamont said, with an urgent and serious tone.

"My sister did have another son," Mrs. Dixie said. The look of surprise was apparent on her son's face.

"Ah hah," Altamont said. "Please continue." Johnson and Dixie leaned forward.

"I had a cousin and never met him?" Dixie asked, somewhat perplexed. Johnson smiled a bit as Dixie said that, seeing this tough man of the streets, now meek-mannered and sounding like a kid in the presence of his mother.

"I'm afraid so," Mrs. Dixie said. "Hattie loved to drink liquor, and take up with all kinds of men, while she was married. Her husband Ben made good money and was always on the boat with his fishing fleet. He left her alone quite often. One night, Hattie got really drunk, just after Ben went to sea, and was staggering home from a bar. A white man, she said, offered to help her home. When he got her inside her apartment, he raped her."

"You never mentioned that Momma," Dixie said.

"Why Steve? What happened to her was grown folks business boy, and you weren't grown folk at the time. She became pregnant and told Ben it was his. She made me promise I would not tell Ben about the rape. I didn't. Months later, her secret was revealed in the most horrible way."

Mrs. Dixie paused, almost as if she was reliving the moment of Hattie giving birth.

"The colored doctor pulled Ronald (The Fixer) out first and smiled as he handed him to me since I was helping him. He told Hattie, Ronald had a twin. Then the doctor's face had the most horrified look as he pulled the second boy out. It was so strange. The second boy was white."

There was a silent pause.

"How was this possible Momma?" Johnson said.

"The medical term for these phenomena is 'Superfecundation' and there are very few reports of this type of birth ever recorded," Altamont said. "Superfecundation most commonly happens within hours or days of the first instance of fertilization with ova released during the same cycle. There is a small time window when eggs are able to be fertilized. Sperm cells can live inside a female's body for four to five days. Once ovulation occurs, the egg remains viable for twelve to forty-eight hours before it begins to disintegrate. Thus, the fertile period can last five to seven days. Ovulation is usually suspended during pregnancy to prevent further ova becoming fertilized and to help increase the chances of a full term pregnancy. However, if an ovum is released after the female was already impregnated when previously ovulating, there is a chance of a second pregnancy—albeit at a different stage of development. Can we assume, Mrs. Dixie, that your sister had relations with your brother-in-law before he went to sea?"

"Yes I would assume so. Hattie complained to me he was trying to get her pregnant with the hopes she would stop drinking. He wanted her to be more responsible," Mrs. Dixie said. "I think he suspected she was taking up with other men when he was gone which is also part of wanting her with child."

Johnson saw Dixie's mind reeling with the revelation of his family's well concealed secret.

"What did they do with the boy after he was born?" Johnson asked.

"Ben was sick with sorrow," Mrs. Dixie said. "He said the most horrible things to her, calling her a harlot, whore and tramp or any other thing he could think up in his rage. He said this was God's punishment to her for being unfaithful to him. He called the white baby the 'devil's work' and saw him as some form of evil unleashed on the world. He knew he could never walk the streets with a colored and white son. People would laugh at him and talk something fierce. He was so ashamed. He wrapped the white baby up in a blanket and left the apartment. When he returned, he said nothing, and no one asked where he took the white child. We all assumed he left the child out in the cold to die. We never heard any report that a child was found, so my sister started believing the child had been tossed in the sea. She was so broken by the whole thing her health soon began to fail her. Ben left her as well. She died a woman full of sorrow and regret. Ben had been good to that woman and when he left her so did the comfortable life he provided her. She was drunk everyday of her life after that. She eventually drank herself to death."

"If my suspicions serve me right, as they have up to now, I suspect the child was not tossed into the sea," Altamont said as he leaned back into his chair. "Thank you, Mrs. Dixie, and I assure you I will try and keep this matter between the four of us. I have a trusted associate who works at Scotland Yard, I will have to share this with him, but he can be trusted to remain silent. Gentlemen, we must leave immediately. I need to investigate this situation further." Altamont shook Mrs. Dixie's hand and stood outside in the night air with Johnson while Dixie took a moment to say a proper farewell to his mother. As Dixie joined the men, Johnson gently grabbed the great detective by the arm.

"How did you do it?" Johnson asked.

"Do what?" Altamont returned.

"How on earth did you come to the conclusion that there was another brother involved and that he was white?" Johnson asked.

"Elementary, my dear Mr. Johnson. The note, I deduced, addressed to the white assailant, emphasized the fact that his brother was at the warehouse. Scotland Yard constables questioned all of The Fixer's men and it was very clear that The Fixer was alone at the warehouse. I could only assume the brother reference was regarding The Fixer," Altamont said. "However, I thought the brother reference may have meant brothers in crime, but The Fixer was shot and lays in the hospital fighting for his life. If they were loyal to each other in crime, why shoot the man? I just followed the feeling I had in inside me Mr. Johnson. That same feeling that has helped me foil the plot of many criminals in the past."

"You okay?" Johnson asked Dixie. Dixie nodded his head but remained silent.

Altamont flagged down a passing hansom.

"I'm off to awaken a friend in the city census department. I'm sure he won't appreciate me paying a visit this time of night but if my hunch is correct, England, and Her Majesty's people are in grave danger," Altamont said. "Where will the two of you be if I need you?"

"At my flat for the rest of the night. Mr. Dixie you're staying with me tonight. We're both tired," Johnson admitted. "I will accompany Mr. Dixie to his 11 a.m. meeting with Inspector McKinnon in the morning."

Altamont thought for a moment.

"With the chain of events that have happened this night I'm afraid I'll have to postpone my trip to Ireland for one more day," Altamont said. "I'll meet you in the morning at Inspector McKinnon's office. Be prepared, Mr. Dixie, for a rigorous interrogation by Inspector McKinnon when you arrive. I suspect he thinks you may have a hand in your cousin's nasty business. Before I continue, I have to ask you Mr. Dixie, are you involved, in any way, with this mess your cousin is caught in?"

The question days earlier would have offended Dixie, but strangely enough, not this time.

"I assure you Mr. Holmes, I have nothing to do with any of this, but for my cousin's sake, I will assist you until we get to the bottom of this."

Altamont climbed in the hansom bidding farewell to the men. Johnson and Dixie decided to walk to Johnson's flat. Johnson knew Dixie had to clear his head. So did Johnson. The day's events had worn both he and Dixie down physically. Johnson was going to make sure Dixie got some rest and be alert for his meeting with Inspector McKinnon in the morning.

Chapter 14

Johnson made sure he awoke early. They both were so exhausted the night before they slept as soon as they laid down. He had insisted Dixie take his bed while Johnson slept on a collections of pillows. He wanted Dixie to visit his cousin before the meeting with Altamont and Inspector McKinnon. When they arrived at the hospital, they found out The Fixer had been moved. The morning sun beamed brightly through the hospital room where The Fixer was taken. Johnson saw Dixie smile and shake his head when the nurse told him that his cousin had been moved to a private area upon the request of his doctor. Johnson knew Dixie's heart was touched when he realized The Fixer was now under the private care of Dr. Watson. As Dixie sat next to his cousin's bed, Johnson knew Dixie wished the young criminal would awake and shed some light on just how deeply The Fixer was involved with this mysterious situation. How did all of it result in a near fatal gunshot wound to the chest? The nurse said The Fixer had gained consciousness several times but was too weak to speak or stay awake for any period of time.

How did this mysterious white brother of his come into play? What was the connection between the two? Where did The Rat fit into all this? Why was the attraction of criminal life in the streets of East London so alluring to both Dixie and his cousin? Johnson wondered would at some point, Dixie's find himself stretched on a hospital bed, if he didn't leave behind the demons of criminality that possessed him? Johnson was so deep in thought he never saw Dr. Watson enter the room.

"A penny for your thoughts, Mr. Dixie?" Dr. Watson asked.

"Good morning Dr. Watson. I guess I was so deep in thought I didn't even hear you come in. My apology," Dixie said.

"Good morning Dr. Watson," Johnson said. He watched Dr. Watson reach for a chair and sit it next to Dixie and share his thoughts.

"I must admit when I first met you at Holmes' residence that day I truly detested you. The mitigated gall you showed that day trying to intimidate Holmes angered me to my very core," Dr. Watson said. "Even when I was reengaged with you in solving Mr. Johnson's case I didn't trust you and really wanted nothing to do with you. But then once I looked past my anger I honestly saw something changing in you in that case. I think you saw through your own eyes how crime hurts people and I think it has effectuated how you'll approach life in coming days."

"Perhaps you have a point," Dixie said. "After we arrested the men who were after Mr. Johnson, and I was leaving Scotland Yard, I felt a burden lifted from my shoulders. I believe at that point I had decided to change my ways. But my cousin's shooting brought me right back into the muck and mire."

"Or at least you think you've been dragged back in," Dr. Watson said. "No Mr. Dixie, had you reacted as the person I first met, you would probably be traveling up and down the East End intimidating people trying to get answers. Instead, you're trying to leave behind that old self, and you have aligned yourself with Holmes and Scotland Yard to solve this case. Had you gone haywire in your underworld networks, bashing heads to gather information, and not find or accomplish anything, all you would have succeeded to do would be to scare the culprits into permanent hiding."

Johnson smiled and nodded his head in agreement with Dr. Watson. But before Dixie could reply, The Fixer's weak voice became audible.

"Water, water," The Fixer said as his eyes barely opened. Dr. Watson poured a glass of water and went to his patient's side, gently placing the glass to The Fixer's lips and urging him to sip slowly. Dixie circled quickly to the other side of the bed and clasped his hand into his cousin's.

"Who did this to you cousin, who shot you?" Dixie asked with a desperate tone. His cousin raised his eyes ever so slightly and recognized it was Dixie. He began whispering.

"Find Tank cousin, find Tank," The Fixer instructed before drifting back to sleep.

"He has gained consciousness like this off and on since I've been on the case," Dr. Watson said. "But this is the first time he has ever spoken. Dixie glanced at his pocket watch and realized he had just enough time to make his 11 a.m. meeting with Inspector McKinnon.

"I have a meeting at Scotland Yard with Inspector McKinnon and I believe Mr. Holmes will be there as well. I'll be sure to let them know my cousin said to search for a bloke named Tank," Dixie said as he shook hands with Dr. Watson.

"I'm right with you Mr. Dixie," Johnson said and the duo dashed out of the hospital, excited that they had a solid lead to share with the two lawmen. After instructing the hansom driver where to take them, Johnson watched Dixie lay his head back. Johnson could tell the pressure of the last few days were wearing on Dixie.

Johnson and Dixie walked into Inspector McKinnon's office and immediately, Johnson saw citations of commendation, on the walls for the investigative accomplishments Inspector McKinnon achieved over the years. Johnson wondered how many of those cases had actually been solved by the great detective sitting across the desk.

"Good to see you again Mr. Johnson and Mr. Dixie. I'm impressed. You are right on time," Inspector McKinnon said. "Mr. Holmes just started briefing me about the meeting with your mother last night, Mr. Dixie. I assure you that whatever is shared here in this room will stay in strict confidence between the four of us. Continue Mr. Holmes." Johnson and Dixie shook hands with the inspector and then Holmes before taking a seat. Holmes resumed talking.

"As I was explaining to Mr. Dixie and his mother last night, and to give you the short version for time sake inspector, Superfecundation occurs when a woman has sex with two different men within a short period of time, and two eggs are fertilized at the same time, as a result. The first recorded case was made by John Archer, an American physician in 1810. According to Archer, a white woman who had sex with a colored man and a white man within a short time period subsequently gave birth to twins—one white, one of mixed-race," Holmes said. "I believe this is what happened in the case of The Fixer and his yet to be located white brother. I believe this scenario is the crux of this case. We find The Fixer's brother and we get to the bottom of this complex situation. Whatever the criminal activity turns out to be, I believe Her Majesty's country is at risk."

Dixie could withhold his information no longer.

"Mr. Johnson, Dr. Watson and I were at my cousin's bedside this morning just before we came here," Dixie added. "He awoke just briefly, just long enough to tell me to find someone named Tank. Inspector McKinnon, I'm hoping you may have a photo in your files of someone with that nickname. Perhaps if we find Tank, we can solve this situation."

Holmes however reacted as if a bolt of lightning had struck him.

"Why of course," Holmes said.

"What is it?" Inspector McKinnon asked. He saw the look on Holmes' face in many cases before. The great detective was on to something.

"I found a document on the floor when we were searching The Fixer's warehouse, Inspector McKinnon. It had British military letterhead on it and the name of Ernest Swinton* on it," Holmes said. "I believe you may have given me the missing piece to our puzzle, Mr. Dixie."

Dixie smiled, taking pride in the fact he had helped the great detective.

"Then maybe his nickname is Tank?" Johnson asked.

"No I believe the name has deeper implications. Mr. Johnson and Mr. Dixie, the Army military facility is not too far away. Would you join me in a hansom ride there to do some more investigating?"

The men nodded.

Holmes pulled out a sheet of paper and handed it to Inspector McKinnon. The name Winston McCloud was written on it, with an address.

"Inspector McKinnon, if you would be so kind as to have one of your boys go to this address and find the whereabouts of this person, Winston McCloud?" Holmes asked.

"I will go personally," Inspector McKinnon said. "I can see your keen detective senses are raging, and I want Scotland Yard to have a hand in the solution to this drama."

The hansom ride took the men into a part of England Johnson had never seen before, a secluded area where the British Army military command post was situated. After a one hour wait, a private escorted the threesome to the office of British Army Colonel Ernest Swinton. Swinton watched the visitors' enter. His gaze was that of curiosity as he stood to greet them and shake hands.

"I will be honest, when I heard I had visitors, I verbally raked the private up and down, reminding him that I did not take unannounced appointments," Colonel Swinton said. "But when he mentioned that it was the legendary Sherlock Holmes, I accepted your visit. I've been a great fan of yours for quite some time and he knew that. Good kid that private. How can I help you Mr. Holmes?"

"To receive accolades such as that from a man of your stature, Colonel Swinton, is indeed an honor. However, I hope you feel the same about me after I pose this question," Holmes said with a serious tone. "How in the world did a man as capable as you, allow sensitive Army military intelligence to fall into the hands of some of England's most unsavory characters? Because of your incompetence sir, a man lays in a hospital bed, fighting for his life. Can you explain this to me?"

Colonel Swinton arose quickly and walked to his office door, that had been left slightly ajar, and closed it. His face wrinkled with concern as he took his seat again, trying to remain composed.

"I know of you, Mr. Holmes, but I have no idea who these two men are. I'm not comfortable discussing military business based on this fact," Colonel Swinton said.

Dixie leaned forward and answered with a tone of indignation.

"And I sir, am not comfortable with the idea my cousin is laying in his hospital bed, because you made a dreadful error," Dixie said. Holmes placed a hand on Dixie's arm. During the hansom ride, Holmes had instructed Johnson and Dixie to leave the talking to him. "Sorry, Mr. Holmes."

"This gentleman is Mr. Steve Dixie and he is a trusted associate of mine. I'm allowing him to follow me on this case because he may learn a few tools of the trade and in time become a pretty good private investigator in his own right. I trust him explicitly," Holmes said. "The gentleman beside him is Jack Johnson, the world heavy weight boxing champion. Now Colonel Swinton, if you would, please explain." Johnson watched Altamont slide the military document with Colonel Swinton's name emblazon on top, toward the colonel. Colonel Swinton glanced at the paper but didn't acknowledge it.

"The boys down at the officers club will never believe me. I met the great Sherlock Holmes and the legendary Jack Johnson all in one day," Swinton said, hoping to divert the conversation.

Johnson glanced at Dixie and saw the glee on his face.

The great Sherlock Holmes hated him at first, and now counted him a trusted associate. Not only that, the great detective projected him to have the potential to be a good private investigator. Johnson wasn't sure where all this was going, but Dixie's self esteem had grown immensely this very hour with Holmes' statement.

And while Colonel Swinton tried desperately to change the subject, he knew Holmes' reputation as an investigator. Colonel Swinton knew Holmes was on to him and the military document confirmed that fact. He needed to get in front of this horrid situation and perhaps with Holmes' help he could.

"Mr. Holmes I've been dabbling with an idea that will serve Her Majesty's army in such a great way, but it is still in preliminary stages. I believe it is possible to construct a petrol tractor on the caterpillar principle, armor it with hardened steel plates, and it is my belief that it would be able to counteract heavy fire from machine-gunners," Colonel Swinton said. "This machine that, I would call a tank*, would reach speeds up to five miles-per-hour, have the capability of making a sharp turn at top speeds, it would have the ability to go in reverse, it would have the ability to climb a five-foot earth parapet, and have the ability to cross an eight-foot gap. In addition this tank could house ten crew members, two men on machine guns on either side and one man on a two pound gun."

At the mention of the machine's name, a tank, Holmes looked at Johnson and Dixie. Holmes had felt all along, whatever The Fixer was shot for, could indeed hurt England's during a war. If this information was provided to France or Germany, it would make either of England's rival countries a greater wartime threat. "So what happened to the plans?" Holmes asked.

"Remember now these plans are still in preliminary stages, and I don't think I'll be ready to present it until next year," Swinton said. "Each night, I take the plans home with me, and gradually draw up the specifications for this tank. I would honestly say my specs are three-quarters of the way complete. A few weeks back I stopped at a pub in West London for some drinks with a few of my Army chaps. I was feeling comfortable and having a great time and instead of securing the envelope with the plans in it, I just let it lay free next to me. I went to the bathroom and I believe that was when I got nicked."

Dixie chimed in. "Was the pub called "The Raven" by any chance?"

"Why yes, how did you know?" Colonel Swinton asked.

"My cousin called the pub his moneymaker," Dixie said. "He would spot a drunken aristocrat type, and watch his spending flow at the table or bar. If he saw what he called a mark, he would signal his man outside and they would accost the poor soul when he left the pub."

"So we can deduce that The Fixer had marked the colonel but when he saw an unattended envelope on a table, left by a high ranking officer, he nicked it, without having to confront the colonel," Holmes said. "He probably had a hunch there was something valuable in that envelope and settled for that."

"So you have an idea who may have stolen my plans?" Colonel Swinton asked.

"We're not sure exactly who the thieves are but they are

connected to Mr. Dixie's cousin we're sure of that," Holmes said. "I'm afraid that is all we have to tell at the moment, but we must leave you Colonel Swinton. The trail leading to these scoundrels is hot, we must move quickly."

Holmes and Dixie shook hands with the still nervous colonel and hailed a hansom to Jack Johnson's flat. Before Holmes went in, he sent word to Inspector McKinnon by a patrolling constable, to meet him there.

"Mr. Johnson, we are closing in on the trail of the assailants and we will wait here for Inspector McKinnon," Altamont said.

An hour passed, and there was a tap on the door. Johnson greeted Inspector McKinnon, and let him in.

"Do you have good news?" Holmes asked the inspector.

"Well, Mr. Holmes, I have good and bad news. We searched for a last known address for the name of the Winston McCloud fellow you gave me, but he wasn't there. That is the bad news," Inspector McKinnon said. "However, the man who adopted this Winston McCloud was there. Harry McCloud is an Irishman who moved to England many years ago, and owned and commanded a fishing boat for a living. He is getting up in years, and for the life of me, I didn't understand why he thought I was there to arrest him. He asked me, 'what took so long'?"

Holmes shook his head, knowingly, as he sat in a chair and lit his pipe.

"I assume he thought you were there to arrest him. The boy he adopted did not come from the birthing source he falsified on the adoption document and filed when adopting the boy, correct?" Holmes said.

"You scare me sometimes when you do that, Mr. Holmes, but yes, you are correct. It seems one evening, one of his colored ship mates came to his home with a newly born white male baby. The colored shipmate would not tell him initially from where the baby came, but he assured the man the child was unwanted. Harry McCloud's wife, it seems, was barren and could not have children. He and his wife saw this child as a gift from heaven, because they desperately wanted children. It seems Mr. McCloud paid an adoption official a rather tidy sum, under the table, to get him to falsify, and then approve the boy's adoption."

Johnson was struck by the irony. To the black family, the white baby was the devil's work. But to the white family, he was a gift from heaven. Every situation in life was a matter of perspective he thought.

Dixie grunted.

"So my uncle-in-law could not bring himself to take the child's life, so he gave my cousin's brother away to a white family," Dixie concluded.

"Correct, but not just too any white family, but one that he trusted. Here's the strange thing. On occasion the colored fellow, who gave McCloud the boy, would drop by to see how the child was developing. By now, old man McCloud knew the truth. It seems that without the men's knowledge, the boy overheard their private conversations about the origin one day when he was older. This is how the boy found out he had a colored mother and brother," Inspector McKinnon said.

"This Winston McCloud, followed the colored fellow to his home one day, and discovered what his fraternal brother looked like. He obviously met and spoke with his colored brother and from there they became pretty close and met many times. Harry McCloud said he was surprised one day to come home and find the colored brother in the living room with Winston and his wife. They told him they knew everything, but the wife and Winston said they forgave the old man for not telling them directly. They spent a lot of time together after that. That was until Winston joined the French Foreign Legion.*"

"I never heard of the French Foreign Legion," Johnson admitted.

"The French Foreign Legion has been a military service wing of the French Army since 1831," Holmes said. "It is unique because despite the fact the units are commanded by French officers, it was exclusively created for foreign nationals willing to serve in it. Let me guess Inspector McKinnon, since both you and I know The Fixer specializes in dealing weaponry; it is safe to deduce that his brother Winston was his supplier. Correct?"

"Spot on, Mr. Holmes," Inspector McKinnon said. "When I told Harry McCloud what kind of trouble Winston was in, I also assured him if we found the young man without his help, I could not guarantee a safe outcome for young Winston. His wife is dead now and he lives alone. The boy's recent visits have been the only solace he has. He doesn't want the boy to die in a shootout with Scotland Yard. So he gave me the only address he had for Winston. It is a tiny little shack near the boat wharfs, here in East London and beside that sits a storage bin. I made an initial inquiry with the French Foreign Legion, and it seems Winston and three other Legionnaires have been away without leave for over four months. The French Foreign Legion also said a rather large cache of weapons were missing. I assume this shack is where Winston and those men live and they stashed the stolen French Foreign Legion weaponry in that storage bin. I have two constables watching the buildings as we speak, but I thought you might want to be there when we nab the villains."

Dixie spoke. "It is all making sense now. The word on the streets was that my cousin had weaponry for sale, for use in the streets, and quite a few men who really should not have guns are armed on the streets with those black market weapons. I knew my cousin was a thief but I refused to believe he had the resources to be an arms dealer."

"And now Winston McCloud and his new partner in crime, The Rat, have Colonel Swinton's specs for the tank. I am willing to bet they plan on selling them to either the French or Germans for a generous payoff," Holmes said. "Enough, that's if they negotiate well, they will never have to work another day in their lives."

"Tank? Did you find this guy Tank?" the inspector asked with great enthusiasm.

"I'm afraid inspector that Tank is not a who, but more so, a what," Holmes responded. Holmes went on to tell the inspector about the visit to Colonel Swinton's office and about the almost completed specifications for a weapon that could counteract hunkered down machine-gun nests. And he told how they were stolen.

"We have to get there right now," Inspector McKinnon said after hearing the details. "Mr. Holmes you suspected this matter had Her Majesty's kingdom's national security at risk, and you were right. It is uncanny how you see these things."

Holmes merely nodded his head, snuffed the ashes in his pipe, and along with the three men left in haste for the shack.

Epilogue

As Johnson led the men onto the street adjacent to his flat, the last face he expected to see was that of Alphonse Capone. The look on Capone's face was one he had seen many times before, at the end of one of his prize fights. It was an expression of utter defeat. If Capone's look wasn't an indication, that something dreadful had happened, then the bleeding and unattended gash on the left side of his forehand spoke volumes. Johnson stopped dead in his tracks. The other men came to an abrupt halt, as well, when they saw Capone. The teenage mobster could barely raise his eyes to meet Johnson's as he spoke.

"Tex Cody escaped, Mr. Johnson," Capone said.

Frankie Yale emerged from a hansom, directly after Capone broke the bad news. He soon stood beside Capone. The look on his face was embarrassment. Upon hearing this news, Johnson felt a rush of exhaustion course through his body. He dropped to one knee, in a crouch, seemingly too tired to remain standing.

Altamont and Inspector McKinnon stepped forward, Altamont placing a hand on Johnson's shoulder, while in the same instance, the inspector addressed the teenagers.

"What happened?" Inspector McKinnon asked.

"We did as you instructed Inspector McKinnon. We were accompanying Inspector Youghal in escorting the two South Africans and Cody back to America. When we arrived at the *Mauretiana*, we were told to wait dockside. The two South Africans had to relieve themselves so Inspector Youghal took them to a nearby bathroom. He asked Frankie to go with him, and I was told to watch Cody," Capone said. "There were several passengers there with us. For the life of me, I never saw a weapon on any of them, and quite frankly, I think I was just looking forward to going home. Before I knew it, Cody had his arm around a passenger's neck and obviously withdrew a gun he had spotted in the man's waistband. Cody had all of the passengers, including me, to lay flat on the ground. When Inspector Youghal and Frankie returned, Cody, with the gun now pointed at the man's temple, made the inspector give me the keys to the cuffs. Cody made the inspector, the South Africans, Frankie and all the other passengers jump into the water. He made me uncuff him and told the guy he held hostage to jump in the water as well. Then he bashed my forehead with the butt of the gun and held it to my head, with the trigger cocked."

"Why didn't he pull the trigger?" Johnson asked.

"I played the only card I had, Mr. Johnson, Cody's fear of the Mafia. I remembered how he reacted, when he heard Frankie's name, in the room last night. I told him Frankie had some powerful friends in the New York and Chicago syndicates. If he returned to America after killing me, Frankie would make sure my murder was avenged," Capone said. "Then I reminded him that there were close ties between the American mob and the Italian Mafia. I told Cody if he stayed in Europe, Frankie would use those connections in Italy, to have assassins hunt him down, and kill him anyway. Instead of shooting me, he hit me in the forehead again with the gun, and ran. I was too dazed to chase him."

Johnson mustered enough strength to stand. "What do

we do now?" he asked Altamont.

"Time is of the essence, in both situations, Mr. Johnson," Altamont replied. "We'll split into teams. Inspector McKinnon, Mr. Dixie and I will follow our original plan to try and prevent The Rat and Winston McCloud from selling the plans for the tank. Mr. Yale, Mr. Capone and you should search for Tex Cody."

"Where do we start searching for Cody?" Johnson asked.

"If I were in Cody's shoes, I would want revenge and then find safe harbor," Inspector McKinnon said. "I think he will go after Lady Hebron again."

"True," Altamont said. "But, if my powers of deduction serve me correctly, I believe he will try and find Lucille. She was the one that lead us to Cody in the first place."

"I remember in the hansom ride on the way to Cody's flat, Lucille mentioned she worked a particular area of the docks a great deal," Johnson said. "She told me I should look for her there if I wanted company. The thought of doing so never crossed my mind; however, even I have a cut-off point as to the type of woman I'll bed down."

There was a round of chuckles shared among the men.

"Then that is where I suggest the three of you start," Altamont said.

"Mr. Capone, what did Inspector Youghal do, once he and the prisoners were retrieved from the water?" Inspector McKinnon asked.

"They changed into dry clothes and still made it in time to get on the *Mauretaina*," Yale said. "They are on their way to America. Al and I wouldn't go. We were sent to England to protect Mr. Johnson and he is still in danger. We will protect him. Plus, Al and I have some New York mafia style plans for this Mr. Cody when we finally catch up with him."

Johnson watched Altamont, Inspector McKinnon and Dixie hail a hansom to go to the shack at the dock to find Winston McCloud and his associates. Meanwhile, Johnson beckoned for a hansom and along with Yale and Capone climbed in, anxious to find Lucille.

Johnson asked the hansom driver if he was familiar with the area of docks where prostitutes worked. The driver knew the area well, and after Johnson told him the threesome had to get there quickly, that it was a matter of grave importance, the driver rode madly through the streets to get them there.

"What else did you say to the driver, to get him to drive like this?" Capone asked.

"He recognized me from previous rides," Johnson said with a smile. "I tip quite well."

When the men arrived and stepped out of the hansom, true to form, Johnson paid and tipped the driver well. "I may need you, please wait right here."

The threesome walked towards the dock, and were met by two women, obviously ladies in the same profession as Lucille. One lady asked if they were "looking for some company."

"We're looking for Lucille," Johnson answered.

The other lady, a beautiful colored woman, looked Johnson up and down, and then gave glances at the teenagers. "Lord child, Lucille will be worn out if she takes the three of you on at the same time. Why not let us in on the party?"

"We don't have time for this," Johnson said, gruffly. "Have you seen Lucille?"

"Well she sure is popular today. Some white American bloke with a weird accent asked about her too," the white woman said. "He found her and took her over behind the crates further down. I thought that was weird, because Lucille has a room, not too far away, that she uses. He looked desperate and in a hurry. I guess that is why he took her there."

"Did he look like someone beat him up with brass knuckles?" Capone asked.

"He looked in bad shape. Someone really roughed him up, looked like to me," the colored woman replied.

Johnson and the teenagers ran at full sprint to the area of crates where the women pointed. Lucille lay motionless on the ground when they found her. Her throat was bruised and discolored from Cody's attempt to strangle her. Yale placed his ear to her mouth, she was still breathing. Something or someone must have kept Cody from finishing her off. Just then, a few yards away, a moan could be heard. The men walked over and found a man laying on the dock surface, bleeding from the head. It was not Cody.

Capone knelt and lifted the man so he lay against a shipping crate. "What happened, sir?"

"I was coming to visit Lucille," the man said. "I heard a scuffle behind the crates and when I got there, a man was strangling her. I tried to stop him but while I was struggling with him, he pulled out a gun, and hit me in the head."

Johnson called the two women over to the crime scene, instructing one to stay with Lucille and the man, while telling the other, to find a patrolling constable. The men ran back to the hansom. No words were exchanged. They all knew one thing was sure. Cody was on his way to Lady Hebron's home.

Johnson gave the hansom driver Lady Hebron's address. "Hurry, man, a woman's life is in danger." The driver pushed his horses to move swiftly through the streets of London, cracking his whip on their backs, urging them to run harder. The men arrived at Lady Hebron's home. Again, Johnson paid the driver and told him to wait. The men made their way to a row of shrubbery just yards away from Lady Hebron's front door. It was dark inside, except for the glow of a dim light in the hallway. They saw a shadow cross the lighted area. It had to be Cody. Johnson wondered if Cody had found Lady Hebron.

"Looking for someone?" a voice asked. The men turned, startled, expecting to see Cody, with his gun leveled at them. It was Lady Hebron.

Johnson leaped from his crouched position and embraced the woman. Capone and Yale did the same. Their hearts were lighter now. They knew she was safe, at least for the moment.

"How did you get out?" Johnson asked.

"I heard someone prowling around, outside, when I was in my upstairs room," Lady Hebron said. "I looked out from my window, and saw that damn Cody. I put on my dressing gown and slippers and ran down to my basement. The previous owner had built a secret passageway from the basement that leads outdoors. I was hiding, and then I saw the three of you. Cody is inside the house by now. I heard him break a window, when I was descending the steps to the basement."

"He is inside the house," Johnson said.

"Mr. Johnson, stay here, with Lady Hebron. Frankie and I will go inside," Yale said. "We know he has a gun. The odds aren't in our favor walking in there bare-handed."

Lady Hebron left the men and returned. In her hand she held a revolver and butcher knife. "I keep these in the drawer next to my bed. I grabbed them when I left. I decided if I had to confront him, I wanted to be outside, in the open, where I had room to shoot him. If I missed, I hoped to gut him like a fish," Lady Hebron said.

Johnson smiled. "I'm in love with you Lady Hebron."

"Make that all three of us," Capone said, he too, in full admiration of Lady Hebron's demeanor.

"Enough chit-chat," Johnson said. "Change of plans. Frankie, you keep a watch on the front door. Lady Hebron, show Alphonse and me where to enter the house. Then come back and stay with Frankie. Mr. Yale, when Lady Hebron returns, start talking to Cody. Hopefully that will distract him, while we launch a surprise attack from behind."

Capone shoved the knife safely in his belt, so not to endanger himself. He reached in his jacket breast pocket, pulled out his brass knuckles, and slipped them on. "I'll lead the way in, Mr. Johnson, if anyone takes a bullet, let it be me. If that happens though, you'll only have a few seconds to take Cody down."

Johnson nodded. They followed Lady Hebron to the concealed entry to the house. Before they entered, and Lady Hebron walked back to where Yale was, she gave both men a huge kiss on their cheek. They smiled like school children, and then entered the house. Within minutes, Johnson and Capone ascended the basement stairs and reached the open door. Johnson counted it a blessing that the basement step had been crafted so sturdily, not one board was loose, so there were no noises to be heard as they approached. Johnson and Capone could see Cody peering out the front window. He could hear Yale taunting Cody.

"Hey Cody, if you want Jack Johnson so badly, why don't you drop the gun and come out, and fight him like a man? Oh, that's right, you already tried that, in Texas, and got your ass beat in front of all your friends," Yale said as he laughed loudly. "Oh, by the way, someone out here wants to say hello."

Lady Hebron's voice was clear and distinct. "You idiot, I'm out here. You have got to be one of the dumbest criminals I've ever known."

Cody retreated from his crouch in the window, and stood, visibly angry at what Yale said, but he became even angrier hearing Lady Hebron's taunting voice. Cody shifted the gun to his left, non-shooting hand, and with his right hand began hitting the wall. He was throwing a full-blown temper tantrum. This was the opening Capone needed. The teenager bolted through the basement door, and was on top of Cody, before he could put the gun back into his shooting hand. Both men toppled to the floor. The gun landed several feet away from the men and Johnson picked it up. Capone drove his brass knuckles with a vicious punch into Cody's throat. As Capone stood, Cody lay on the floor, body thrashing, both of his hands on his throat, desperately trying to catch his breath. "Stand him up," Johnson said to Capone.

Capone lifted Cody to his feet and stepped to one side.

Johnson, with his entire force of energy centered at Cody's midsection, connected a punch to the side of the same rib cage Capone had fractured, the night before, at Cody's flat. The howl of pain Cody emitted was frightening. He dropped to both knees. Johnson delivered an equally vicious blow, to the same jaw, that Capone had fractured the night before. Cody's face visibly caved in, from the blow. Cody fell forward, with his face, being the first body part, to make contact with the floor. Cody lay motionless. Johnson didn't check to see if Cody was unconscious or dead. He didn't care. Johnson stepped on Cody's back as he made his way to the front door, letting Yale and Lady Hebron inside the house. Lady Hebron placed her hand on her mouth when she saw Cody's still body stretched on her floor, his head soaking in an expanding pool of blood. Johnson walked towards Cody's body and kicked it. "Get this garbage out of here men. I don't want to know what you do with him."

"Lady Hebron, I know this is a weird question, but would you happen to have any raw fish in the house?" Yale asked. Lady Hebron disappeared into her kitchen. While Lady Hebron was gone, Yale and Capone removed Cody's cowboy designed shirt. When she returned, she handed Yale a butcher's paper with fish wrapped inside. Yale opened it, selected the largest fish, rewrapped the fish, and handed it back to Lady Hebron. While Yale did this, Capone found a newspaper and brought it to Yale. Yale wrapped the fish in Cody's shirt and then wrapped the shirt in the newspaper. Yale handed the package to Johnson.

"Give this to Altamont," Yale said. "We're headed back to the dock. We'll give Mr. Cody a decent Mafia burial."

The teenagers dragged the unconscious Cody to the waiting hansom. While they loaded the body inside, Johnson paid the driver handsomely. "Take them back to the docks. I'm paying extra because I don't want you to say a word about what you witnessed here tonight." The driver nodded and urged his horses to move forward. By chance, Johnson spotted another hansom sitting vacant down the street. "Lady Hebron, I hate to leave you with all that blood to clean up, but I really need to find Altamont and Inspector McKinnon."

"Don't worry about the blood. I'll take pleasure in cleaning it up, knowing I'll never see Cody again. I saw the looks on Mr. Yale's and Mr. Capone's faces, I'm convinced I'm right."

She hugged Johnson again. Johnson ran towards the hansom, the fish wrapped in newspaper tucked safely under his arm.

Minutes later and miles away, at the dock, Yale and Capone unloaded Cody's body from the hansom, and dragged it to the dock's edge where the water was visible below. The two women who were there earlier approached them. They nodded with approval, knowing Cody was the man who tried to strangle Lucille.

"We'll keep our eyes open for a patrolling constable," The colored woman said. "Just make sure this bloke doesn't strangle another woman." The teenagers nodded.

Yale found two cinder blocks while Capone retrieved rope. They tied rope to each cinder block, and then tied the rope to Cody's ankles. Cody began mumbling. He tried to struggle, but realized his hands were tied behind his back.

"Good, you're conscious," Capone said, as he kneeled to look Cody in the face. "As the water fills your lungs, you'll have just enough time to think about what a mistake it was to come searching for Jack Johnson."

The teenagers threw the cinder blocks into the water, and Cody's body followed. They watched him sink into the murky waters.

Part Two

Johnson gave the new hansom driver a vague description of the area of the dock Altamont and McKinnon were headed. He was impressed that the driver knew where he wanted to go. He climbed in, but not before handing the driver a generous amount of money. "I must get there quickly."

The driver drove his team of horses swiftly through the London streets to Johnson's destination. As the hansom pulled up to the dock, a small battalion of British army soldiers were just arriving. Inspector McKinnon spotted Johnson and waved him over.

"Well, did you find Tex Cody?" the inspector asked.

"Yes," Johnson replied. "Where is Altamont, and why is the British army here?"

"Answer my question first, Mr. Johnson," the inspector said with authority.

"Mr. Cody is with Mr. Capone and Mr. Yale," Johnson said. "We decided to handle Cody's situation, American style."

The inspector paused for a moment, trying to determine what that meant. If Yale and Capone were involved, the solution most certainly involved some form of criminal act. But Inspector McKinnon didn't inquire further about Cody. Cody never registered with Scotland Yard, to let them know he was a bounty hunter in pursuit of Jack Johnson. So officially, there was no record of Cody ever being in England. The inspector concluded he had more pressing issues at hand, so he would let the Cody matter rest.

"The army battalion you see, Mr. Johnson, is a part of the force Colonel Swinton commands," the inspector said.

"These men are a special force, specially trained to handle delicate situations, especially when Her Majesty's army has infiltrated foreign soil. Mr. Holmes sent word to the colonel that we located the thieves. Since the culprits are in possession of sensitive British Army intelligence, the matter falls under the colonel's jurisdiction. Follow me. I'll take you to Mr. Holmes, or Altamont, as you so strangely refer to him."

Altamont was perched on a hill over looking the shack, as he peered through a pair of field glasses. Colonel Swinton was beside him. Altamont smiled when he saw Johnson.

"Mr. Capone and Mr. Yale, sent this to you, Altamont," Johnson said, handing the rolled up newspaper to him. Altamont opened the newspapers, recognized Cody's shirt and unfurled it, and lifted the fish in his hand.

"Why in the world would they send you something as strange as this?" the inspector, asked Altamont.

"Would you like to explain, Mr. Johnson, or should I?" Altamont asked.

"They sent it to you, Altamont, you explain," Johnson said.

"In the world of the Mafia, fish wrapped up in an article of clothing, of a person who has been killed, is then wrapped in newspaper and delivered to the Mafia bosses. This act signifies that the person is dead, and at the bottom of the sea," Altamont explained to the inspector. The inspector looked at Johnson.

"Will this ritual come back to haunt me?" Inspector McKinnon asked.

"I doubt it," Johnson replied. "Capone and Yale are pretty good at what they do."

The inspector shook his head, wondering how he got so deeply involved with the American Mafia.

"What's going on down there?" Johnson asked Altamont.

"Since we arrived, there has been a shift change. One man replaced another in front of the storage bin where we are pretty sure the weapons are stored," Altamont said. "The man, who was relieved from guard duty, is inside the shack, seated at a table with a bottle of liquor. We have identified Winston McCloud but there is no sign of The Rat."

Dixie joined the men and exchanged a handshake with Johnson. One of Colonel Swinton's men appeared and whispered in the colonel's ear.

"My snipers are in place, Mr. Holmes," the colonel said.

One moment, before we proceed, colonel," Altamont said, handing Johnson a set of field binoculars. "You need to see this."

As Johnson looked into the shack, he saw McCloud roll up the left sleeve of his shirt, exposing his bare arm. On the table, sat some form of liquid, and McCloud placed the needle end of a syringe in the liquid, and drew it into the syringe's casing. McCloud located a vein on his arm and tied a small piece of rope around the arm, causing blood build up in his arm's veins.

"What in the world is he doing?" Johnson asked.

"Mr. McCloud is about to inject a seven-percent solution of cocaine into his blood stream," Altamont said. "This will make my interrogation of Mr. McCloud, much easier."

Johnson watched McCloud insert the needle in his vein

and push the liquid through the casing, into his veins. McCloud removed the needle and rope and laid his head back. His eyes glossed over into a glassy stare.

"Now, Colonel Swinton," Altamont said. Colonel Swinton gave his snipers the nod, signaling they could shoot at will. The first sniper's bullet pierced the heart of the sentry in front of the storage bin and he fell lifelessly out of his chair, to the ground. The second sniper's bullet entered the right temple of the man seated at the table in the shack and he slumped forward, his head resting on the table. The colonel's men ascended on the shack, with skilled precision, entering the shack and cuffing a non-confrontational McCloud.

"Mr. Johnson and Mr. Dixie, would you accompany me to the shack, please?" Altamont asked.

Johnson saw the colonel's men remove the body from the shack and place it next to the dead man in front of the storage bin. Johnson and Dixie followed Altamont as he entered the shack. Johnson was amazed at the control Altamont seemed to have over the soldiers. Altamont asked the soldiers guarding McCloud to leave. Johnson and Dixie stood at the door while Altamont released McCloud from his cuffs. Johnson noticed the dream-like state in which McCloud seemed to be in. Then Altamont pulled up a chair, so he was sitting alongside McCloud. McCloud did not object when Altamont carefully lifted his arm and observed many needle punctures in the man's arm. McCloud was a cocaine addict. But it was the tone, in which Altamont spoke to McCloud that surprised Johnson. Altamont spoke to McCloud with a voice full of empathy.

"This may surprise you, Mr. McCloud, but I can relate

with you and your addiction," Altamont said. "I too was prone to inject a seven-percent solution* of cocaine on many occasions early in my lifetime. It was a very nasty habit and one that caused a dear friend, to trick me into seeking treatment, with a very famous German psychiatrist*."

Johnson glanced at Dixie, hoping his face did not show the surprise and confusion, apparent on Dixie's face.

McCloud lifted his head, and gazed at Altamont. Johnson suspected that young McCloud did not know he was talking to the great detective, Sherlock Holmes. But it was the mention of Altamont's ability to identify with McCloud that sparked the reaction from McCloud. Altamont pressed on.

"My addiction was driven by pure boredom, during the periods, of which I didn't have interesting cases to investigate," Altamont said.

"But, Mr. McCloud, I believe your addiction is driven by something much deeper. I believe you inject a seven-percent solution because you are trying to run away from something. Perhaps something you did, perhaps you betrayed someone very dear to you," Altamont said. "Have you heard the latest prognosis on your brother, The Fixer? I imagine it has been hard for you, the past few days, knowing you shot The Fixer, your brother, and left him for dead in his warehouse?"

McCloud exploded.

"I didn't shoot my brother. That colored bastard, The Rat, he shot my brother," McCloud screamed. "My brother had the plans in his hand and I was trying to reason with him. The Fixer did not want to give British military secrets to another country. For some reason, my poor colored brother, felt some type of allegiance, to Her Majesty's crown."

Johnson caught Dixie's eye, and shook his head, telling Dixie not to interrupt Altamont. Johnson could only imagine that Dixie was fighting every fiber in his body not to approach McCloud and choke the life out of him. Dixie followed Johnson's silent command, and remained still.

"Is my brother dead?" McCloud asked.

"No, he is not dead. But he is very weak. My friend is his doctor and The Fixer is getting the best medical attention possible," Altamont said. "But tell me, why did The Rat shoot The Fixer?"

McCloud paused for a moment, trying to recount the incident.

"The Fixer had the plans to the tank in his hand. I was trying to reason with him, convince him that we could leave this God forsaken country and start a new life, somewhere else. We would have more money than we could ever imagine. But he wouldn't listen. He said he wouldn't have the lives of his fellow countrymen on his hands because he sold the plans to the tank to our enemy. Then that bastard, The Rat, became too impatient, and shot him. The Rat grabbed the plans from my brother's hand and ran. I didn't know what to do, so I ran too," McCloud said.

"Where is The Rat now? Where are the plans? You will feel much better, Mr. McCloud, if you get this burden of guilt off of your chest," Altamont said.

Johnson saw McCloud look at Altamont, his drug deluded eyes were sad.

"We had bids from Germany and France. Germany finally agreed to pay us double what France was offering,"

McCloud said. "I despise The Rat for shooting my brother; I cannot stand to be in his presence. I sent him with one of my men to meet a German courier at the dock where the *Mauretiana* is usually located to make the exchange. There is a cargo ship sailing for Germany tonight. I told The Rat I never want to see him again, once the deal is completed. My brother and I are going to be rich, sir," McCloud said. Johnson realized the drugs in McCloud's system made the man delusional. McCloud had not fully comprehended that his accomplices were dead, that he was alone, and that he was looking at serious trouble when he appeared in the British Army court system.

"What is the name of the ship, Mr. McCloud? At what ship will The Rat and your man meet the German courier?" Altamont insisted on knowing.

"The *Constellation*," McCloud said.

Johnson saw Altamont spring from his chair and bolt for the door. Johnson and Dixie ran behind him. Swinton's men entered the shack to officially arrest McCloud. They followed Altamont to the top of the hill where Colonel Swinton and Inspector McKinnon were waiting.

Johnson marveled at the change in Altamont's mood. Altamont displayed the characteristics of a bloodhound that had just picked up a fresh scent.

"We must get to the loading dock where the *Constellation* is anchored," Altamont said, still running, as he passed the colonel and inspector. Johnson and Dixie were right behind him. "Bring your best sniper colonel, and inspector, you need to catch up with us."

The men used the smaller military wagons that brought

the colonel's battalion to the shack. During the ride, Colonel Swinton and Inspector McKinnon checked their pistols for readiness. Swinton brought along his best sniper, an officer named Cooper, who had a calm demeanor as he sat next to Johnson. The men arrived at the *Constellation*. As they ran towards the cargo ship, Dixie spotted The Rat with a white man and pointed them out. The colonel instructed Cooper to find a high place where he could shoot from. Altamont, Johnson and Dixie ran behind Inspector McKinnon who had his weapon drawn.

"You two, halt," the inspector barked loudly. Johnson stopped, and ran towards a body that lay in the shadows. The man was dead, as best that Johnson could tell. Johnson figured The Rat was pulling a double cross, and never meant to share the money with McCloud. The dead man was McCloud's man.

When the German courier saw the inspector and Altamont running towards him, he grabbed the pouch containing the tank specifications from The Rat's hand and started running towards the platform leading to the *Constellation*. The Rat went in the other direction towards the water. The Rat was running with a suitcase in his hand. McKinnon fired a shot at the German courier but missed. Colonel Swinton fired a shot at The Rat, but he missed his target as well. The sound of Cooper's sniper rifle pierced the air and the German courier fell forward, dead from a bullet wound to the head. Altamont made it to the German courier's body first. Altamont confirmed the German was dead. Colonel Swinton arrived next, picking up the pouch.

"There's a dead body over there," Johnson hollered to Altamont. I think it is McCloud's man." Johnson spotted Dixie in hot pursuit of The Rat and ran in the direction of Dixie. The suitcase opened while The Rat was running and money began falling out. The Rat stopped and began scooping up as much cash as he could and started running again. Dixie seemed to be gaining on him. The Rat reached the water and dove in. Dixie stopped short, at the edge of the water. Johnson reached Dixie, as he watched The Rat's figure disappear into the dark waters.

"Why didn't you go in after him?" Johnson asked.

"I can't swim," Dixie said with disgust.

Part Three

Inspector McKinnon walked into the lobby where Johnson was waiting with Altamont and Dixie.

"The Germans deny knowing anything about a German courier," the inspector said. "When we gave them his name, they said he was a rogue agent, who they kicked out of their intelligence community several years ago. They also deny knowing anything about allocating a large sum of money for his use."

Johnson shook his head. America had disavowed knowledge of many American agents who were caught spying in a foreign country. It was all standard procedure for the world's intelligence communities.

Johnson was surprised, however, when he saw Dr. Watson walk into the lobby. The doctor went directly to Dixie.

"Your cousin passed away over one hour ago. I did everything I could, Mr. Dixie," Dr. Watson said.

"I know you did," Dixie said, consoling the doctor.

Johnson walked to Dixie and placed a comforting hand on his shoulder.

Dixie looked at Altamont and shook his head sadly.

"Mr. Holmes, what you said in Colonel Swinton's office, the other day. Were you serious? Would you help me get on the right side of the law?" Dixie asked.

Altamont looked at Johnson, then Dixie.

"If you are serious, and willing to renounce your passion for criminal life, I can share some investigative tips with you," Altamont said.

"Why are you asking?" Johnson inquired.

"Because I won't rest until I bring The Rat to justice," Dixie said.

Endnotes:
Chapter 1

*On July 12, 1912, black boxer Jack Johnson opened the Cafe de Champion.

*In the story "His Last Bow", we learn that Sherlock Holmes, in the character of an Irish-American named Altamont, has infiltrated a German spy-ring in Britain. No specific dates are given, except for the conclusion of the story, which takes place on the second of August 1914. Holmes tells Watson: "When I say that I started my pilgrimage at Chicago, graduated in an Irish secret society at Buffalo, gave serious trouble to the constabulary at Skibbareen [in Ireland], and so eventually caught the eye of a subordinate of Von Bork, who recommended me as a likely man, you will realize that the matter was complex." It seems probable that Holmes could have been in Chicago in 1912.

*June 9, 1946: Jack Johnson is killed in an automobile accident outside Raleigh, North Carolina.

*Johnson was a fugitive for seven years, having been accused of violating a white slavery act with a woman who would become his third wife.

*Johnson was charged with taking Lucille Cameron across state lines for "immoral purposes," a violation of the Mann white slavery act. With the charge hanging over him, Johnson married Cameron on Dec. 4, 1912.

Chapter 3

*The **White-Slave Traffic Act**, better known as the **Mann Act**, is a United States law, passed June 25, 1910 (ch. 395, 36 Stat. 825; *codified as amended at* 18 U.S.C. §§ 2421–2424) It is named after Congressman James Robert Mann, and in its original form prohibited white slavery and the interstate transport of females for "immoral purposes". Its primary stated intent was to address prostitution, "immorality", and human trafficking; however, its ambiguous language of "immorality" allowed selective prosecutions for many years, and was used to criminalize forms of consensual sexual behavior.

*In 1869, again near the banks of the Orange River, a Griqua witch doctor named Swartbooi found an 83.5 carat stone, a brilliant white diamond, nicknamed the "Star of Africa," on the Zandfontein Farm, owned by two Afrikaner farmers, Diederik De Beers and Joahannes De Beers. Niekerk heard of the stone, and traded nearly all his possessions, including 500 sheep, 10 oxen, and a horse, to the young man for the stone. He sold the diamond to the Lilienfeld brothers for 11,000 pounds sterling. The brothers then sold it to the Earl of Dudley for 30,000 pounds sterling, sparking the diamond rush to South Africa.

* The word **kaffir**, sometimes spelled **kaffer** or **kafir**, is an offensive term for a black person, most common in South Africa and other African countries. Generally considered a racial or ethnic slur in modern usage, it was previously a neutral term for black southern African people.

Chapter 4

* "Mark" – It was customary for teams of people to identify someone with money and then rip them off.

* The **Siege of Sidney Street**, popularly known as the **"Battle of Stepney"**, was a notorious gunfight in <u>London's East End</u> on January 3,1911.

* Steve Dixie first appeared in "The Three Gables." He was a black boxer and a member of a criminal gang, the Spencer John gang. Holmes indicates that Dixie was responsible for "the killing of young Perkins outside the Holborn Bar." Holmes generally holds Dixie in disdain: some of his remarks have been interpreted as racist, though they were probably really inspired by the fact that Dixie is a crook and a pugilist, who tried to intimidate Holmes. Dixie is the only black male character to ever appear in a Sherlock Holmes adventure.

Chapter 6

* There were actually two black character ever depicted in the Sherlock Holmes stories. The first to appear is Lucy Hebron, in "The Yellow Face." The chronologists disagree about the date of this particular story, placing the events in various years between 1881 and 1888. Lucy, the daughter of a black American father and a white English mother, is a little girl at the time, probably no older than five, so at the period when this story takes place she would be about thirty-five.

* Jazz is said to be a variation of the word "jism," because it was originally performed by horn players to entertain johns in the whorehouses of Storyville, the notorious red-light district of New Orleans. The problem is that no bands played in the whore houses; pianists, yes, often behind a screen or curtain. Bands played in saloons and dance halls only. Contrary to popular belief/accepted wisdom, it was what was playing downstairs on a piano when one lost that last shred of innocence, not a loud group of musicians. Trombonist Clay Smith was rumored to have said, "If the truth were known about the origin of the word 'jazz,' it would never be mentioned in polite company."

* Earl Hines one of jazz's most influential musicians, said that he was playing this style of music on the piano around his native Pittsburgh "before the word 'jazz' was even invented."

* The original B Street Irregulars were a group of fictional characters featured in the Sherlock Holmes stories. They were a group of street urchins who helped Holmes out from time to time. The head of the group was called Wiggins. Holmes paid them a shilling a day (plus expenses), with a guinea prize (worth one pound and one shilling) for a vital clue. They first appeared in Conan Doyle's original Sherlock Holmes story, _A Study In Scarlet_ (written 1886, published 1887). They also appear in the next novel, _The Sign of the Four_; one of the chapters from this book is called _The Baker Street Irregulars_. Like Holmes in this adventure, many were up in age which prompted Altamont to say he had to look for them and explains why he needed Dr. Watson's help.

Chapter 7

* According to Johnson's 1927 autobiography, he married Mary Austin, a black girl from Galveston, Texas, in 1898. No record exists of this marriage, and the 1900 census shows him still living at home with his parents and siblings. Although they were probably never legally married, Johnson introduced Austin as his wife wherever he went. She was the first "Mrs. Jack Johnson."

* During the summer of 1903, Johnson met a black prostitute named Clara Kerr at a North Philadelphia whorehouse. In September of that year, she traveled with him to Bakersfield, California, and was his companion for much of the next three years. In October of 1906, she ran off with an old friend of Johnson's, a racehorse trainer named William Bryant. She took most of Johnson's jewelry and clothing as well. Johnson tracked the couple down to Tucson and had Kerr arrested on burglary charges, but Johnson and Kerr reconciled for a time. They moved to California, but Johnson was having trouble finding moneymaking fights, and when the money ran out Kerr left him again — this time for good.

* Ford began the production of the Model T car using an assembly line. From 1913 to 1927, about 15 million Ford Model T's were built, making it the second most produced car in history, behind the Volkswagen Beetle.

* Born in Italy, Frankie Yale and his family arrived in America around 1901. As a teenager, Yale quickly fell into a life of crime. Despite his medium height and chubby build, Yale was a fearsome fist fighter and thief. In 1910, at age 17, Yale and a friend of his, a wrestler named Booby Nelson, beat up a bunch of drunks in a Coney Island pool hall, cracking pool cues and hurling billiard balls. One of his early arrests, in October 1912, was for disorderly conduct. Early in his career, Yale met Johnny "The Fox" Torrio, who ushered him into the Five Points Gang and groomed him for bigger things.

* Capone's life of crime began early. As a teenager, he joined two gangs, the Brooklyn Rippers and the Forty Thieves Juniors, and engaged in petty crime. Capone left school in the sixth-grade at age 14, after being expelled for punching a teacher at Public School 133. He then worked at odd jobs around Brooklyn, including in a candy store and a bowling alley. After his initial stint with small-time gangs, Capone joined the notorious Five Points Gang, headed by Frankie Yale. It was at this time that he began working as a bartender and a bouncer at Yale's establishment, the seedy Harvard Inn.

* One story is that when he was working as a waiter for a young couple, he leaned down and said to the woman, "Honey, you have a nice ass and I mean that as a compliment." Her brother, Frank Gallucio, pulled a knife and slashed Capone in the face three times before leaving the bar with his sister. Word of the fight eventually reached Yale, who forced Capone to apologize to Gallucio.

*Another story is that he asked a Sicilian barber to give him a particular style of haircut popular with Sicilian gangsters and the barber refused (perhaps because Capone was a Neapolitan), upon which Capone vandalized the shop, knocking down a row of personalized shaving mugs belonging to customers and the barber then slashed his face with a straight razor.

* Racial **passing** refers to a person classified as a member of one racial group attempting to be accepted as a member of a different racial group.

Chapter 8
* Back in New York during his younger days, Al Capone went to work for Yale tending bar and even supplying muscle at Yale's Harvard Inn at Coney Island. Yale tutored Al on the ways of gangstering. Yale was said to be sometimes kind, but was also known as very wicked.

Chapter 9
***April 1909:** Johnson meets Belle Schreiber at Chicago's Everleigh Club.

***April 19, 1909:** Jim Jeffries announces that he will come out of retirement to attempt to win back the title from Johnson.

* **October 1909:** Johnson meets Etta Duryea at the Vanderbilt Cup car race on Long Island.

* **June 25, 1910:** President William Howard Taft signs the

White Slave Traffic Act, better known as the Mann Act, into law. It bans the transportation of women across state lines "for the purpose of prostitution or debauchery, or for any other immoral purpose."

* **January 18, 1911:** Johnson and Etta Duryea are married in Pittsburgh.

* **July 4, 1910:** Before a crowd of 12,000 people in Reno, Nevada, Johnson defeats Jim Jeffries and retains the heavyweight title.

* **July 4-5, 1910:** Johnson's victory spawns race rioting all over the United States. At least 26 people are killed, and dozens are injured.

* **November 2008:** Barack Hussein Obama was elected the first black president of the United States.

Chapter 10
* In the adventure "The Abbey Grange" it opens with Holmes waking Watson on a cold morning, and saying:
"Come, Watson, come!" he cried. "The game is afoot. Not a word! Into your clothes and come!"

* And "Wisteria Lodge" includes a sentence:
"As impassive as ever to the casual observer, there were none the less a subdued eagerness and suggestion of tension in his brightened eyes and brisker manner which assured me that the

game was afoot."

Chapter 11

* To outsiders, Five Points was a frightening slum; from the inside it was a thriving working-class neighborhood. Named for the points created by the intersection of Park, Worth, and Baxter streets, the neighborhood was known as a center of vice and debauchery throughout the nineteenth century. Outsiders found Five Points threatening and fodder for lurid prose.

* Born in Galveston, Texas, one of seven children, Jack Johnson dropped out of school after fifth grade and began to do odd jobs around town. He began training to box after beating up a local bully and by 1897 had become a professional boxer. It is inconclusive that Tex Cody could have been that bully.

* Inspector McKinnon appeared in "The Retired Colourman" c. 1898. Youghal (rank not mentioned at the time) was consulted by Holmes in the "Mazarin Stone" c. 1903.

* RMS *Mauretania* was an ocean liner ocean designed by Leonard Peskett Leonard and built by Swan, Hunter & Wigham Richardson, Tyne and Wear Swan, for the British Cunard Line, and launched on 20 September 1906. At the time, she was the largest and fastest ship in the world.

Chapter 12

* Frankie Yale's gang was engaged in a battle for control of union activity on the Brooklyn docks. They were successors in a war that had been going on since the turn of the century between

Italian Black Handers and the incumbent Irish, who had banded together to form a rival gang calling themselves the "White Hand". Frankie arranged for the murder of White Hand leader Dinny Meehan, which took place on the afternoon of March 31, 1920. Several weeks later, on May 11, 1920, longtime Chicago boss James "Big Jim" Colosimo was also murdered. Chicago police suspected Yale committed the hit at the behest of Chicago Outfit pals Torrio and Capone. Colosimo was allegedly murdered because he stood in the way of his gang making huge bootlegging profits in Chicago. Although never charged with the Colosimo murder, Frankie Yale was the prime suspect.

* In 1925, Capone became the Chicago crime boss when Torrio, seriously wounded in an assassination attempt, surrendered control and retired to Brooklyn. Capone had built a fearsome reputation in the ruthless gang rivalries of the period, struggling to acquire and retain "racketeering rights" to several areas of Chicago. That reputation grew as rival gangs were eliminated or nullified, and the suburb of Cicero became, in effect, a fiefdom of the Capone mob. Perhaps the St. Valentine's Day Massacre on February 14, 1929, might be regarded as the culminating violence of the Chicago gang era, as seven members or associates of the "Bugs" Moran mob were machine-gunned against a garage wall by rivals posing as police. The massacre was generally ascribed to the Capone mob, although Al himself was then in Florida.

*June 27, 1914: Johnson takes on Frank Moran at the *Velodrome d'Hiver* in Paris. After 20 lackluster rounds, Johnson is declared the winner. The next afternoon, Archduke Franz Ferdinand of Austria-Hungary is assassinated in Sarajevo, starting the chain of events that triggers World War I.

Chapter 13
* The first recorded case was made by John Archer, an American physician in 1810 and is discussed in *Williams Obstetrics* (1980). According to Archer, a white woman who had sex with a black man and a white man within a short time subsequently gave birth to twins—one white, one of mixed-race. This is similar to some incidents of mixed twins.

Chapter 14
In August 1914 the British government established the War Office Press Bureau under F. E. Smith. The idea was this organization would censor news and telegraphic reports from the British Army and then issue it to the press. Lord Kitchener decided to appoint Swinton to become the British Army's official journalist on the Western Front. Using the pseudonym, *Eyewitness*, Swinton was instructed to write articles about what was happening on the front-line. Swinton's reports were first censored at G.H.Q. in France and then personally vetted by Kitchener before being released to the press.

Swinton worked to strict guidelines. He was not allowed to mention place names or soldiers' battalions, brigades and divisions. Swinton was told that no article could be passed for publication if it indicated that he had seen what he had written about. He was also instructed to write about "what he thought was true, not what he knew to be true".

When observing early battles where machine-gunners were able to kill thousands of infantryman advancing towards enemy trenches, Swinton wrote that a "petrol tractors on the caterpillar principle and armored with hardened steel plates" would be able to counteract the machine-gunner."

Swinton's proposal that the British Army should build what he called a tank was rejected by General Sir John French and his scientific advisers. Unwilling to accept defeat, Swinton contacted Colonel Maurice Hankey who took the idea to Winston Churchill, the navy minister. Churchill was impressed by Swinton's views and in February 1915, he set up a Landships Committee to look in more detail at the proposal to develop a new war machine.

The Landships Committee and the newly-formed Inventions Committee agreed with Swinton's proposal and drew up specifications for this new machine. This included: (1) a top speed of 4 mph on flat ground; (2) the capability of a sharp turn at top speed; (3) a reversing capability; (4) the ability to climb a 5-foot earth parapet; (6) the ability to cross a 8-foot gap; (7) a vehicle that could house ten crew, two machine guns and a 2-pound gun.

* The French Foreign Legion was created by Louis Philippe, the King of the French, on 10 March 1831. The direct reason was that foreigners were forbidden to serve in the French Army

after the 1830 July Revolution, so the foreign legion was created to allow the government a way around this restriction. The purpose of the foreign legion was to remove disruptive elements from society and put them to use fighting the enemies of France. Recruits included failed revolutionaries from the rest of Europe, soldiers from the disbanded foreign regiments, and troublemakers in general, both foreign and French. Algeria was designated as the foreign legion's home. The army was formed so the government could enforce its rule in Algeria.

Epilogue
* In *A Study of Scarlet,* the first book in which Sherlock Holmes appears, there was an indication he may have been a drug user.
" . . . for days on end he would lie upon the sofa in the sitting-room, hardly uttering a word or moving a muscle from morning to night. On these occasions I have noticed such a dreamy, vacant expression in his eyes, that I might have suspected him of being addicted to the use of some narcotic, had not the temperance and cleanliness of his whole life forbidden such a notion."

* In *The Sign of Four* the notion that Holmes was an addict became more evident.
Sherlock Holmes took his bottle from the corner of the mantel-piece and his hypodermic syringe from its neat morocco case. With his long, white, nervous fingers he adjusted the delicate needle, and rolled back his left shirt-cuff. For some little time his eyes rested thoughtfully upon the sinewy forearm and wrist all dotted and scarred with

innumerable puncture-marks. Finally he thrust the sharp point home, pressed down the tiny piston, and sank back into the velvet-lined arm-chair with a long sigh of satisfaction.

Then, later in *The Sign of Four*, Holmes admits his usage.

"It is cocaine," he said, "a seven-per-cent solution. Would you care to try it?"

* In the *Seven Percent Solution*, German psychiatrist, Dr. Sigmund Freud treats Holmes' addiction.

Also From MX Publishing

Winners of the 2011 Howlett Literary Award (Sherlock Holmes book of the year) for '**The Norwood Author**'

From one of the world's largest Sherlock Holmes publishers dozens of new novels from the top Holmes authors.

www.mxpublishing.com

Including our bestselling short story collections 'Lost Stories of Sherlock Holmes' and 'The Outstanding Mysteries of Sherlock Holmes'.

New in 2012 [Novels unless stated]:

Sherlock Holmes and the Plague of Dracula
Sherlock Holmes and The Adventure of The Jacobite Rose [Play]
Sherlock Holmes and The Whitechapel Vampire
Holmes Sweet Holmes
The Detective and The Woman: A Novel of Sherlock Holmes
Sherlock Holmes Tales From The Stranger's Room
The Sherlock Holmes Who's Who [Reference]
Sherlock Holmes and The Dead Boer at Scotney Castle
The Secret Journal of Dr Watson
A Professor Reflects on Sherlock Holmes [Essay Collection]
Sherlock Holmes of The Lyme Regis Legacy
Sherlock Holmes and The Discarded Cigarette [Short Novel]
Sherlock Holmes On The Air [Radio Plays]
Sherlock Holmes and The Murder at Lodore Falls
Untold Adventure of Sherlock Holmes
Sherlock Holmes and The Terrible Secret

Also from MX Publishing

Sherlock Holmes Travel Guides

London   Devon

In ebook (stunning on the iPad) an interactive guide to London

400 locations linked to Google Street View.

Also from MX Publishing

Cross over fiction featuring great villans from history

  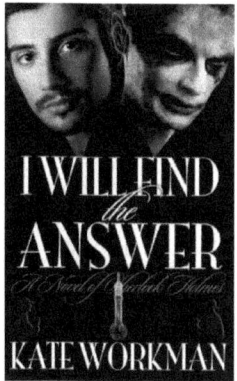

and military history Holmes thrillers

 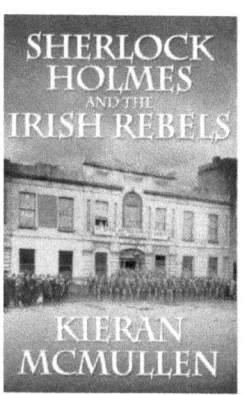

Also from MX Publishing

Fantasy Sherlock Holmes

And epic novels

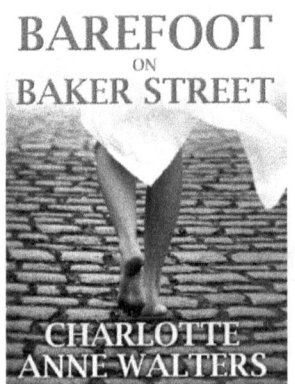

Links

The Anomalous publication date was deliberately put in Sherlock Holmes Week to raise awareness for Save Undershaw – the campaign to save and restore Sir Arthur Conan Doyle's former home. Undershaw is where he brought Sherlock Holmes back to life, and should be preserved for future generations of Holmes fans.

Save Undershaw   www.saveundershaw.com

Sherlockology   www.sherlockology.com

MX Publishing   www.mxpublishing.com

You can read more about Sir Arthur Conan Doyle and Undershaw in Alistair Duncan's book (share of royalties to the Undershaw Preservation Trust) – An Entirely New Country and in the amazing compilation Sherlock's Home – The Empty House (all royalties to the Trust).

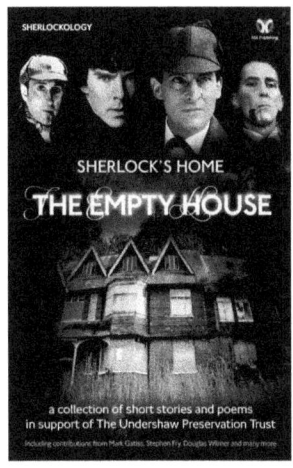 

www.ingramcontent.com/pod-product-compliance
Lightning Source LLC
Chambersburg PA
CBHW071700090426
42738CB00009B/1599